zechoslovak First Republic

1939

18

OLYMPIA publishing house in cooperation with the Museum of Decorative Arts in Prague

Elegance of the Czechoslovak First Republ

Czech Fashion

1918·1939

Eva Uchalová

Deposits of the Museum of Decorative Arts
were used in the publication.

The book was co-written with
PhDr. Helena Jarošová
(The Beginnings of Fashion Design and Drawing)
PhDr. Josef Kroutvor
(A Tribute to the Czechoslovak First Republic)
Jan Mlčoch
(Photography and Fashion in the Intermezzo
of the Two World Wars)
Petr Štembera
(Advertising in the Czechoslovak First Republic)

ISBN 80-7033-425-8

A Tribute to the *Czechoslovak First Republic*

František Drtikol, Portrait of Tomáš Garrigue Masaryk

Time is fortunately not measured by the number of years, but by the intensity of being and meaning. The Czechoslovak First Republic lasted only two decades which, set next to the almost completed modern century, is not a long time. Despite this, the First Republic represents in our modern history a basic term, as it is a measure of fulfilled time.

The First Republic carved a deep trace in the nation's consciousness which even survived the long period of the totalitarian regime. The First Republic established a democracy with a developed legal system, and also developed a selfsufficient economy and independent culture. The characteristic typical of the First Republic was, above all, humane tolerance, the weakness and strength of democratic principles. The new republic did not only bring a change of regime, but also a more modern arrangement of existing conditions. The First Republic meant more than just a political change; the new form of the state was also an attempt to establish a new moral orientation for the nation.

For Czechs and Slovaks, Western style democracy was a completely new historical feature. With the First Republic, the two nations reached the level of modern Europe. The National Awakening of the last century had awakened the soul of the nation, but it was only the First Republic which gave birth to its spirit and gave the nation a deserved self-confidence. Julius Firt writes at the end of his memoirs: "No, I don't want to draw a false picture. Our First Republic had its problems. But what human creation does not have these? It had its narrow-minded censors, who nevertheless only served the popularity of the censored. It had its scandals of corruption and its 'political pathological sediment', as TGM put it. It had great and unavoidable unemployment and great human poverty. But who here or abroad has thus far managed to abolish these? And it had many other things which cast shadows on its image. Nevertheless, the spots of light prevail. Especially that great flowering of culture, illuminated by freedom's rays, and the humaneness of the relationships between people of various professions, views, religions, and various political orientations". This is not only

a speech about the First Republic; it is said by a new person, a citizen of the republic.

Tomáš Garrigue Masaryk („TGM"), the first president of the republic became its symbol. His personality is often connected with morality, reliability, tolerance, and spiritual qualities. Thus a certain kind of officiality, a certain civil pathos, a norm of thinking and behaviour was developed. The idea of the state more or less concerned every citizen, because everybody was in fact a citizen. The three first letters — TGM — perfectly represented the informal officiality of the spirit of citizenship. In all places where the letters TGM appeared, there was a seriousness which was not only an official seriousness. Such citizens' conception of morality has a certain special feature in itself that we can hardly understand today. People were truly proud and self-sacrificing. The First Republic lived in both history and in people's hearts.

It does not seem that the First Republic was only shrouded in seriousness; it was also able to enjoy itself and to conduct a rich social life. The First Republic liberated social life, giving entertainment free reign. Finally, it was not necessary to pretend anymore, to express oneself in allusions and with the aid of hidden meanings. From this liberal feeling a social satire emerged which was a certain kind of continuation of social life. Humour became a public thing. Humour belongs to democracy, and we could say that it was also characteristic of the citizen of the republic. We can hardly imagine the First Republic without the Osvobozené divadlo, a theatre which was the top institution of humour, poetry, and satire. The First Republic certainly did not lack elegance, ingenuity, respect, culture of speech, a sense of honour, and optimism... Already at the beginning of the 1920s, the democracy created its own specific artistic style, a Czech variation of Art Deco. From the disintegrating Cubism, which was complemented by decorative curves, architects created new and unusual forms.

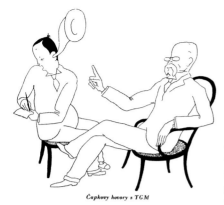

Čapkovy hovory s TGM

Drawing by A.Hoffmeister

Rondocubism, a specifically Czech style, combined the post-war decorativism with abstracted elements of Czech folklore, national ideas, and symbols of state. In this sense, the building of Gočár's Legiobanka on Poříčí street is unique, and it represents a textbook example of the style from the first years of the new republic. Legionnaries were present at the foundation of the Czechoslovak state, and it is therefore understandable that they strove to create a monument that would go beyond the usual kind of bank palaces.

Kysela's painted decoration of the Legiobanka building features the three national colours, and its decorative patterns are often inspired by folk ornaments. It was indeed František Kysela, among other things also the creator of the state coat-of-arms and president's flag, who significantly contributed to the transformation of Art Deco into an official style. Czech Art Deco gave its best efforts to serve the state. Even Czech banknotes were executed in the style of Art Deco, and thus the building, state, and money form a unique unity. However, the attempt to develop an independent Czech style eventually only reached a dead end. The development of modern architecture and lifestyle quickly lost national accents and sentiments and quickly reoriented itself in the direction of the international language of uncompromising modern 'isms'.

In 1922, the twenty-seven year old Ferdinand Peroutka published an essay called *Jací jsme* (Who we are), a meditation on Czech tradition. Peroutka critically evaluated the old Slavism and declare himself for the democratic principles of Western Europe. Old myths were being destroyed and decorations from the last century were being removed. Other voices joined Peroutka, and people began to work systematically, breathe freely, and live. In 1924 Peroutka began to publish the independent weekly *Přítomnost* (also helped by Masaryk's generous financial support). The first years of self-denial and post-war difficulties ended, and the real spring of the First Republic began.

Starting in 1925, a group of people from the cultural, intellectual, and political elite met at the villa of the Čapek brothers in Vinohrady in Prague. The meetings started at 5:00 on Fridays. Black coffee was served, no alcohol was drunk, and no cigarettes were smoked. Karel Čapek presided as facilitator. The gathering of men was filled with an atmosphere of intellectual sobriety and moral respect. Among the regular visitors were Fráňa Šrámek, František Langer, the historian Josef Šusta, the philosopher J. B. Kozák, the philologist Vilam Mathesius, the chief editor of the *Prager Presse* Arne Laurin, Karel Poláček, Vladislav Vančura, the economist Josef Macek, and the politician Edvard Beneš. A special armchair was reserved for president Masaryk, which in his absence

Pátečníci

J. B. Kozák, F. Peroutka, K. Kraus, J. Čapek, F. Kubka, V. Vančura, J. Kopta, J. L. Procházka, T. G. Masaryk,
V. Mathesius, J. Šusta, K. Poláček, J. Macek, Fr. Langer, K. Čapek, E. Beneš, A. Laurin, J. Kodíček

Drawing by A. Hoffmeister

remained empty. The participants of the sessions called each other by surname, to which Masaryk liked to add the guest's profession. The respect and admiration for Masaryk was not once accompanied by bewilderment as the debates still had a semi-official character. Only after the departure of the head of the state did the discussion become relaxed. The gentlemen lit cigars and alcohol appeared on the table. They stopped thinking in terms of concepts and began to enjoy themselves.

It appears that Čapek's pragmatism fit well with Masaryk's realism — the Friday meetings generally affirm this. Masaryk supposedly liked the meetings, which perhaps reminded him of an English club and its tradition. From his conversations with

Masaryk Čapek produced a very interesting book, *Hovory s TGM* (*Conversations with TGM*). The book of course is not only a record of the Friday debates but has a wider philosophical basis. The first part of the book was published already in 1929; the second appeared in 1931; and the third in 1935. The trilogy is thus the record of a nine-year conversation, and no journalist would have ever conducted such a long interview. The book is a tribute to Masaryk, and thanks to Čapek. In fact, if this book did not exist, the First Republic would not have become that which it became, that, which it still is.

In 1927, the "Společenský klub" (Social Club), a new center of cultural and social life, was opened in Na Příkopě street. The honorary secretary of the club was the professor Bohumil Markalous, who was known as a writer under the pseudonym Jaromír John. In addition to social norms, John also required a cultivated form of behaviour. Nothing at the club was left to chance — the interior was designed to the very last detail, including the copper ashtrays in the toilets. The new feeling of life created a new lifestyle. The club and social rules perfectly harmonised with the interior decorations.

The creation of a smaller dinner club, the legendary "Tafelrunda", was connected to the "Společenský klub". The club was formed in the hot summer of 1932, most of all for friendship and entertainment. The "Tafelrunda" was a somewhat different gathering than were the Friday meetings held at the Čapek villa, but this group also has its irreplaceble place in the life of the First Republic. In the "Tafelrunda", intelligence was not only a matter of intellect, since human talent as such also played a role there. Any interesting person who attracted the attention of the club could become a member of the group. Women were permitted to attend the "Tafelrunda" but were never accorded a full membership in the group. There was but one exception, and this was the actress and writer Olga Scheinpflugová. The participants of the "Tafelrunda" correctly thought that one family member was fully enough — when Karel Čapek after his marriage requested membership, he was not accepted! Not to accept such a well-known person was quite a gesture — only the "Tafelrunda" could afford such jokes. Club meetings were attended by

Ferdinand Peroutka, Karel Poláček, Voskovec, Werich, Eduard Bass, the old Jan Herben, Jan Masaryk, Karel Steinbach, Čapek's Kadelík, and Julius Firt.

The pre-war avantgarde sympathised with the left. The "Společenský klub" also more or less maintained this tendency to the left. The political parties closest to the club were the Social Democrats and the National Socialists. The "Společenský klub" was based on the democratic platform of the First Republic; functions were only honorary. One of these recognised personalities was Ferdinand Peroutka.

Regarding the atmosphere of social life, Peroutka later expressed himself in this way: "I do not doubt that 'Tafelrunda' helped to form each one of us, as our surrounding environment usually does. It taught a somewhat healthy skepticism and served as a criticism of the "Self", which otherwise would have wanted to grow too great. Furthermore, it was a school for light lifestyle which stayed with some even though the bad times that followed."

Jiří Voskovec and Jan Werich

The year of 1929 is considered to have been the height of economic prosperity. Prague was transformed into a modern metropolis. The year 1929 witnessed the greatest wave of immigration; Prague attracted people even with its high social level, elegance and luxury. New architecture using iron, concrete and glass changed the appearance of the city, as did the presence of advertisements, large billboards, and coloured posters. The Osvobozené divadlo theatre began in 1927 as a small students' theatre with a revue of poetic and exotic skits, parodies, and grotesque scenes. The success of the Vest Pocket Revue was so great that within two years the small theatre was able to move to a large modern hall with a thousand-seat capacity in Vodičkova street. This also is evidence of the unusual, fast-growing social mood of those years in the most fortunate period of economic prosperity. Such a large step of course changed the small theatre into a first class social institution, where the period and its problems were openly commented on. Furthermore, Ježek's music could be heard, and on the posters appeared V + W, the legendary pair of modern clowns. The songs of Jaroslav Ježek united people, from tramps to intellectuals — all went with the times. In the autumn of 1930 Peroutka began to write the first lines of *Budování státu (The Building of the State)*, the basic constitutive work of the First Republic. We should not forget about yet another important centre of cultural and social life, which was the Lucerna palace. With his open-minded conception, the builder Havel understood the need of the period and created a unique modern complex. The big Lucerna hall, for many years the biggest social hall in Prague, was opened already before Christmas 1920. In 1929, Lucerna was joined by Barrandov, another work of the Havel family of entrepreneurs. Barrandov, as a symbol of the new lifestyle, struggled to combine the advantages of a city lifestyle with the grace of nature, and to offer people a new pleasant environment. Only a few other cities could have afforded such romantic luxury combining natural scenery with elegance, social prestige, and energy.

Enormous interest in architecture, applied arts, aesthetics of environment and fashion was typical of the First Republic, and it was in accord with requirements of taste and quality. The establishment of Družstevní práce, Krásná jizba, the existence of outstanding magazines — all that belongs to concrete expressions of cultural-educational efforts, which were a part of a wider democratic programme. The first half of the 1920s was still under the sway of middle-class decorativism, in which people drew their inspiration from French influences. However, in the second half of the 1920s the cultural structure of the society changed significantly. Culture reached not only the high but also middle classes. Czechoslovakia reached the level of the most advanced industrial states in Europe, the republic built, created, and formed. The somewhat cold, functional, and hygienic style deprived of decorative elements, included into its aesthetics a requirement of social standard. Functionalism of the 1930s introduced a novelty which is now called "design" and is nowadays considered a common part of culture.

If we page through the magazine *Žijeme* published by Družstevní práce, for example, we are struck by its high quality. How it is possible that a magazine so well composed and printed appeared at a time when the first signs of the world economic crisis were already apparent? It seems that democracy had a strong core and was not just a utopia. The culture of the First Republic was directed toward the elite, but its support undoubtedly was among the middle, working classes. Czechoslovak functionalism abandoned the outdated notion of a national style and courageously declared itself for the international currents of the interwar avantgarde. The small but democratic country practically identified itself with functionalism and changed it into a vivid example of how both to build and to live. Fashion was also a specific expression of the social and psychic consciousness of culture, although to be elegant did not necesarrily mean to be fashionable. Especially men's styles had more concrete social inspirations, as elegance was also a moral obligation. Acts and behaviour were closely related to clothing. Men's fashion was a condition for the creation of the elite. In 1929 Štorch-Marien took over the Aventinum publishing house, publisher of *Gentleman* magazine, and transformed the magazine into a prestigious social publication. Among the contributors were Kisch, Poláček, Hoffmeister, the historian Novotný, Nezval, Biebl, Karel Čapek, Olga Scheinpflugová, Eisner, Šíma, Urzidil, Adolf Loos, and Elie Faure. *Gentleman* was an eighty-page magazine of the modern man; its graphic design by František Muzika and perfect print complemented this outstanding act of publishing.

On the pages of *Gentleman*, literature and politics naturally mixed with fashion and social life; tourism, motorism, and hiking was recommended. Elsewhere, the magazine recommended mixed drinks or practical sport outfits. Among frequent topics were a man's word of honour, men's responsibility, fair-play, and the behaviour of a genuine man. All articles had a characteristic grace, a light feuilleton style was employed, and the French expression "baisse" frequently used. Each article was in a sense a guide — the *Gentleman* magazine wanted to be and indeed was a school of life. The profile of a Czech gentleman, maybe somewhat starched, was retouched with reflections concerning a slight crumpliness, elegance, and sophisticated social conversation. Such a magazine was a novelty in the Czech lands, and through its pages the society of the First Republic society presented itself in all its glory.

Convinced democrats such as Dr. Štěpán Osuský, Czechoslovak ambassador to France, were chosen as example of real modern men. Osuský was just forty years old. The male forty-year-old served as a symbol of success. Most of the men from the Friday meetings at the Čapeks' were in fact around forty, and Masaryk himself once remarked that he justly felt to be one of them, because forty times two is just eighty. The forties were considered to be a period of elan and productivity. It was an age of adulthood and justified self-confidence, an age of maturity and full independence — simply put, an age marked by characteristics for which the young republic strove.

The Czech gentleman was by no means merely fashionable figure; he was a real person, a living man. The magazines *Žijeme*, *Gentleman*, *Eva*, and also *Pestrý týden* represent the best of the best. They were unique phenomenona of the period in question. The first issue of *Pestrý týden* was released on November 2nd, 1926, and its front page reminded readers, not by a mere chance, of the October anniversary of Czechoslovak independence. Here also can be seen the founder of the state, the president Tomáš Garrigue Masaryk, as well as the three letters TGM. The editor-in-chief of the magazine was Jaromír John, a great promoter of social life. He later also hired Milena Jesenská, an energetic journalist, brave woman, and later famous friend of Franz Kafka. The painter František Tichý made his rich contribution to the design of *Eva* magazine. František Zelenka gave his professional answers to questions regarding home furnishings in the pages of the same magazine.

Elegant social life reached its heyday between the years 1928 and 1933. Later came only its denouncement, the restriction of democracy, and finally its destruction. Already in 1934 the Czech avantgarde renounced constructive tendencies and lost its spirit of optimism. In the same year, a surrealist group was founded in Prague. Anxious states of consciousness appeared on the surface. Ideology began to pervade social and cultural life, and European democracy came to an end. Tomáš Garrigue Masaryk died on September 14th, 1937, and Karel Čapek on December 25th, 1938. The society that relied on Masaryk's humanistic ideals and expected general tolerance experienced bitter dissapointment. Even so, the First Republic represents a tradition which cannot be given up and which well deserves a tribute.

J. K.

Emil Weiss: Fashion house DANDY
Coloured litograph. Printed by Melantrich,
Prague 1929, inv. no. GP 10559

Adina Mandlová in the film Kristián. Toilette from the Hana Podolská fashion house. 1939

The Czechoslovak Woman
between the Wars

The period of the First Republic brought the fulfillment of the emancipatory efforts of several previous generations of Czech women. The political leadership of the new Czechoslovak state expressed its attitude towards the women's issue in its programme statement, the so-called Washington Declaration promulgated on October 18, 1918: "Women will enjoy the same political, social, and cultural rights as men." This policy was later anchored in the constitution with the words: "Privileges of race, gender, and profession are not recognized..."[1] Despite this clear formulation, however, a long and difficult struggle was necessary to translate this program into practice. This is perhaps the reason why so many clubs were founded that united women according to their social and political orientation, as well as their professions and interests. In 1922 the attempt to concentrate these fractured groups led to the establishment of the National Council of Women, which united more than fifty women's associations that existed in the Czechoslovak Republic at that time. The aim of the council was to promote the acknowledgment of the dignity and respect of women, to bring about their equality with men in the areas of education, employment rights, and equality of working conditions, the attempt to increase the influence of women in political decision-making, and the general ethic improvement of society.[2]

Throughout the existence of the National Council of Women, F. F. Plaminková was at its head. An elementary and middle school teacher in Prague, she was a long-time passionate advocate of women's emancipation, a member of a number of feminist organizations abroad, and, from 1925, a senator serving in the national parliament for the National Socialist Party.

The first success in politics was the acknowledgment of both the active and passive electoral rights of women with a law promulgated in 1919 — 1920. In spite of this, the partici-

pation of women in the political life of the new republic increased only slowly. Women became mayors of communities and were candidates in elections to the National Assembly, but their numbers were still low — in the elections of 1929 14 women were given mandates as members of parliament and senators, which was still only 3% of the total number of seats in the National Assembly.[3]

The new era opened to women new opportunities of education and employment. Before the First World War, only two schools of Charles University — the schools of medicine and humanities — had been open to women. The first women graduates were PhDr. Marie Baborová in 1901 and MUDr. Anna Honzáková in 1902. The other institutions of higher learning — the school of law and all technical schools — accepted women only after the change of political regime in 1918. Statistics from that period show that young women made use of their new opportunities: while in the 1927 — 1928 school year 25.7 % of high school students were female, by 1936 — 1937 this number had increased to 34.77 %; at pedagogical high schools the percentage of female students was even as high as 55.87 %. In the academic year 1921-1922, 6.86% of a total of 25,580 university students were women; by 1937 — 38, 16.95 % of a total of 26,000 university students were women.[4]

Young women were able to continue their education after their school-leaving examinations — in 1936 they graduated from short-term courses in pedagogical institutions; schools of arts and crafts; the state music conservatory; business courses at the business schools, complemented by instruction in languages and stenography; courses for the textile industry and care-giving; as well as from a year-long course at the state

Portrait of Františka Plamínková
Eva, February 1st, 1935

Students of the two-year business school Gremium in Prague, 1926

school of economics. Graduates of these courses and schools found employment as teachers
in schools of various levels and kinds, as business and offices workers in both the public and
private sectors, in health-care, agriculture, etc.
A special case was the area of health and social
care that developed after 1918. In 1935 three
schools existed that specialized in the education
of social workers. Graduates of these schools
were employed by health and social institutions,
clinics, and dispensaries.[5]

In the 1920s women's employment in various
professions was closely folllowed by women's
magazines. In 1928, for example, they noted the
first female attorney and associate professor at
the school of law. The designation of a woman
as an associate teacher of Catholic religion in
Brno was regarded as a great success.[6]

The list of university studies open to women
and their employment after graduation, published in 1936, reveals the penetration of women
into all areas — they could work as high school
teachers; in scientific institutes; as doctors, attor-
neys, judges, notaries, lawyers in public, private,
and foreign service; as agricultural specialists,
managers, consular officials in
embassies; as chemical engineers
in enterprises and factories; as
architects, designers, and entrepreneurs; as employees in insurance and health institutions; as
painters, sculptors, etc.
University study in construction
and electro-technical engineering
was open to women, but pro-
spective female students were
warned that these branches still
employed the least number of
women and that women in engi-
neering were still hired with great distrust.[7]

Portrait of Charlotte Garrigue Masaryková

Women attained the highest qualifications in
their fields of study. In 1934 there were several
associate professors at the Prague university,
and there was even a female full professor on
the faculty of the medical school in Bratislava.
In the 1930s a woman claimed a high administ-
rative function: MUDr. Marta Krupičková-Joha-
novská was named ministerial counsellor at the
ministry of health.[8]

At the same ti-
me, even wo-
men in the lo-
west position
of housekeeper
were given ge-
neral acknow-
ledgment in so-
ciety. In 1930
housekeepers
united in the Union of Czechoslovak Housekeepers, whose purpose was to promote the moral
mission of women in the family and to insure
technical training for all tasks demanded by
a modern household. Housekeepers worked in
commissions "for research and rationalization of
households", "for professional questions of hou-
sekeeping", "for consumer and employer questions". They tried to persuade businesses to maintain cleanliness and hygiene. A questionnaire in
the pages of *Eva* magazine regarding household
helpers was also associated with this work. A result of this poll was the training of young household helpers provided by a center for unemp-
loyed youth.[9]

In civil law, one of the first laws of the
new state abolished the requirement
of celibacy for women employed in the
public sector and also acknowledged
their right to the same salary as men.
The new law made divorce easier —
so much so that it was later criticized
for the fact that divorced women and
their children were not sufficiently socially secure.[10] In 1929 women demanded reform of the civil code, demanding that no differentiation be made
between children born in and out of
wedlock. They also demanded that records of illegitimate births be erased from the
public register.[11]

Efforts for education and the attainment of professional qualifications were important features
of the modern emancipated woman. At the
same time, emphasis was put on her moral qualities as well. The example of T. G. Masaryk, felt
throughout society, was for women complemented by the example of his wife, Charlotte Garrigue Masaryková, who was admired and respec-

ted for her wisdom, nobility, and courage, qualities that had been especially in evidence in the period of opposition to the Austro-Hungarian monarchy. The same moral prestige was later enjoyed by the wife of the second president of Czechoslovakia, Mrs. Hana Benešová, who stood by her husband's side from 1909. Like Mrs. Masaryková, she suffered persecution and imprisonment for the political activities of her husband during the First World War. Later, as the first-lady, she had to face the spiritual suffering associated with the Munich Agreement and the occupation of the Czechoslovak Republic by the Germans.

The character of the Czechoslovak modern woman was formed in the conditions of the fortunate symbiosis of the political, economic, social, and cultural development of the young state which created the conditions for the full unfolding of women's individuality. The period demanded refinement in all areas of women's lives. Characteristics which women gained through their involvement in professional and social life, such as accuracy, responsibility, practicality, and political and economic engage, were also valued.[12]

The modern age also called for a harmonious personality. Thus, intellectual and moral qualities were accompanied by the development of physical culture cultivating health, strength, and beauty. The beauty of the human body, the artistic expressive movement, and intellectual values came together in modern expressive dance, which was practiced at a number of dancing schools in Prague represented by names such as Milča Mayerová, Anka Čekanová, Jarmila Kröschlová, and Jožka Šaršeová. They choreographed their dances in cooperation with outstanding designers such as Jaroslav Horejc and the architect František Zelenka, using motifs from contemporary music. The cult of the body in conjunction with expressive dance expressed itself in the gradual shedding of layers of

Students of the dancing school of Jarmila Kröschlová, Eva, May 1st, 1934

clothes, from simple hints all the way to the half-naked bodies of dancers during their performances in Lucerna and the Rokoko theatre. Also cultivated with enthusiasm was social dancing, in which one exotic name followed another, until in August 1926 *Gentleman* magazine claimed that the Charleston was ruler of the dance floor.

Secondary school students at the Sokol rally in 1938, Eva, June 1st, 1938

Rhythmic exercise, propagated by Eliška Bláhová, director of the Girls' Academy in Brno, was a widespread form of physical culture. Gymnastics in the interpretation of Bela Friedländerová — a multi-faceted sportswoman, organizer of womens' sport and social life, publicist, who also profited from a two-year study trip to the

JAKÝ JE ROZDÍL MEZI ŽENOU

běžné společenské úrovně	vnitřně ušlechtilou
Dohovoří se několika jazyky	ovládá dokonale svoji mateřštinu
Dovede popěvovat všechny moderní šlágry	zná také klasiky
Je horlivá vlastenka	neuráží nikdy příslušníka jiné národnosti
Dovede vzdělaně mluvit	dovede včas mlčet
Obleče si na plovárnu parádní prádlo	nechodí ani doma v roztrhaných punčochách
Miluje voňavky	dává přednost vůni čistého, denně koupaného těla
Je sportovkyní duší tělem	ví kromě toho také, kdo byl Rousseau
Hledí pro děti nashromáždit peníze	snaží se je správně vychovat
Hlásá zásady demokracie	nedá své služebné pocítit třídní rozdíl
Dovede dokonale zacházet s růžem a krášlícími prostředky	dává přednost individuálnímu výrazu svého obličeje
Nevyčítá si malou nevěru	nedovede žít v nedůstojném manželství
Je s to, pod přísahou říci úplnou pravdu	nemluví nikdy jinak, než pravdu
Nevykonaný slib se snaží různě omluvit	dodrží vždycky dané slovo
Přichází na schůzky vždycky pozdě a vždycky udýchaná	neopozdí se ani minutu a je vždycky klidná
Oslovuje svého muže ve společnosti s úsměvem	chová se k němu i doma jako k nejdražšímu člověku na světě
Podporuje veřejnou dobročinnost	pomáhá, i když to nikdo nevidí
Je ráda originální	nepřekročí nikdy meze
Má ráda společnost	nikdy nepomlouvá
Snaží se všemožně obelstít i křticí list	nechává klidně a s pocitem vyrovnanosti šedivěti své vlasy R. J.

Eva, April 1st, 1935

"Mrs. Junková in her Bugatti racing car took a great position in last year's race in Plzeň", Elegantní Praha, April 1925

U.S.— also grew in popularity. Sokol, established in 1862, remained the organization of physical education with the greatest mass involvement. The organization's rallies were not only celebrations of physical culture, but also political demonstrations of the unity of the young state.

Sport was a favourite part of the life of Czech women and girls already before the First World War. Summer and winter sports, cycling, ball games, and tennis became more or less accessible to the working middle class of young women. The young generation discovered a new, unmediated relationship to nature which was manifested by the spread of water sports and hiking. Especially popular were canoe and kayak trips on Czech and foreign rivers in connection with camping in the open nature. Camping grew in popularity and weekend log cabins sprouted near large cities. It was especially in this environment that a new ideal of girl and woman was formed — the model of a friend and partner for a man who regardless of the situation was happy, direct, and uncomplicated.

In the 1920s, women took up sports that had previously been reserved for men. The first Czechoslovak women pilots appeared, and automobile driving became popular and widespread among Czechoslovak women. The famous Czech race driver, Eliška Junková, finished her outstanding racing career with victory in the most difficult car race in Europe, the Targa Florio, in 1928. A year later, after the death of her husband, the race driver Čeněk Junek, she quit her racing career. However, automobile sport still attracted women who achieved exceptional results: in 1933 Mrs. Elstnerová, together with her husband, crossed the Italian Sahara, Southern Tunisia, Algeria, and Southern and Western Morocco. The "Blue team" consisting of six Czech women, mostly wives of industrial entrepreneurs, undertook a car trip to Africa in order to promote the quality of Czechoslovak cars. Motorcycles also attracted the interest of Czechoslovak women. They not only rode in sidecars, but also learned how to drive motorcycles and even to race on speedways.

This activity also introduced a new aesthetic ideal: a beautiful woman was one who was athletic, young-looking, slim, firm, with short hair and a tan. Sunbathing was one of the features of a modern lifestyle, and it was done with such passion that an author of an ironic article in *Mésíc* magazine compared it to baking a goose in an oven.[13] Holidays in the countryside and occasional trips to the Adriatic became affordable even for the middle classes.

The mood of optimism of the successfully developing young state, the vision of a happy future with opportunities for education, personal independence, professional and social fulfillment for women began to cloud over in the 1930s. The loss of illusion among the young generation was expressed by Olga Schieszlová in *Eva* magazine in 1938: "We will have to limit our standard of living, though we have always heard that it is desirable to raise it. We see the growth of poverty,

Miss Kovářová, speedway racer.
Eva, June 1st, 1933

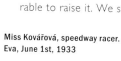

though we have always hoped that it will be abolished. We see arguments, though we have always been taught the victory of concord. We see the domination of material power where we expected the victory of spirit, and the shadow of war is growing larger, though we were raised to have faith in humanity, morality, and hope for a lasting peace among civilized people. We are passing from a bright and rich youth full of faith into a life of uncertainty, deprived of the most beautiful dreams."[14]

The first reason for this disillusion was the economic crisis which brought the problem of unemployment. One of the proposals for the solution of this problem was to bar women from state and public service, a proposal further supported by the decreasing birthrate which, according to economists, was caused by the excessive number of employed women. This proposal contradicted the whole sense of the emancipatory process and challenged some of its successes, and thus provoked a wave of opposition in the wo-men's movement. Nevertheless, with time the proposal was pushed through. After the occupation of the Sudeten lands in 1938, the measure was even extended to private enterprises in order to provide for Czech refugees from the German occupied areas.[15]

Eva, cover by Vojtěch Michal, June 1st, 1933

The second reason for the loss of optimism was the political situation. The fear that peace in Central Europe might be threatened appeared already at the beginning of the 1930s in conjunction with political developments in Germany. With the passage of time, this feeling grew ever more intensive, but it only slowly evoked a determination to act. At first Czechoslovak women expressed themselves politically: at the congress of the International League for Peace and Freedom in Luhačovice in 1937 they rejected the notion of a neutral state. They justified their position with the need for the human solidarity of all nations, collective security, and the indivisibility of peace. At the same time, brochures on topics such as *Woman and Defense*, and magazine articles appeared which advised people how to act in the case of an attack, how to store food, how to create provisions, and how to run a household under conditions of war. On July 1, 1938, the National Council of Women published an appeal in *Eva* magazine for women to look for positions according to their abilities and possibilities for the defense of the state, to attend courses of the Czecho-slovak Red Cross, to become members of civil fire brigades or members of Motorized Defense Corps, to give blood, to organize neighborhood watches of well-trained and calm women, or at least to accustom themselves with precautions against chemical attacks.

The time of the Munich conference and the subsequent occupation of the Sudeten lands in September 1938 provoked great political and practical action in women's organizations. The National Council of Women sent appeals to related organizations throughout the world, to personalities in political and cultural life, to president Beneš and his wife Hana. They wrote that Czechoslovak women were prepared for the "sacrifice of blood, lives, and possessions", and called on the government not to accept the dishonourable conditions of the Munich accord.[16] They sent warnings to the world that the sacrifice of the Czechoslovak Republic would not keep peace. Nevertheless, the Munich accord was signed and immediately put into effect. Czech frontier areas were occupied and tens of thousands of Czech inhabitants had to leave for the remaining territory of the republic. On September 28, the day of St. Wenceslaus, a patron saint of the Czech lands, the National Council of Women published a declaration: "Truth prevails — love prevails! At Easter we turned to you with the slogan 'Truth prevails'. We insist with unshakeable faith in its validity, though it now appears threatened by brute force. Today

we add to it the slogan 'Love prevails'. Both the greatest sacrifice and small actions of everyday life, blessed with love, remain an eternal value. Let us put aside selfishness of all kinds, let us only think of that which is common to and unites us all. Never before have unity and love of all people of good will been more necessary. Let us be brothers and sisters, let us be one family. Strong and determined, let us strengthen and help each other with advice, actions, and understanding. As our President-liberator said, 'Love, liking, is the greatest moral force — from it comes all mutual sympathy, help, and cooperation'".[17]

E. U.

SALON PANÍ ZDENKY ŠUBRTOVÉ
PRAHA II., Václavské n. 42, Palác Hvězda.
Večerní plášť brokátový kombinovaný černým sametem a lemovaný činčilou.

Evening overcoat from the Zdenka Šubrtová fashion house, Elegantní Praha, January 1924

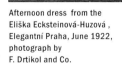

Afternoon dress from the Eliška Ecksteinová-Huzová , Elegantní Praha, June 1922, photograph by F. Drtikol and Co.

ZE SALONU PANÍ ANNY MASÁKOVÉ,
Vinohrady, Fochova tř. 10.
Plesová toileta z bílého crêpe-samothrace, protkaná zlatem a stříbrem (sl. R.) (obuv Slemr, Praha).

D. Armaredo Palacio Waldés:

HŘÍCH LASKAVOSTI.

Ze španělštiny přeložil Dr. V. Jiřina.

Byl jsem tehdy mlád, a dlel jsem návštěvou u staré, neobyčejně chytré dámy. Přišel tam také pán elegantního chování a pyšného, domýšlivého obličeje. Paní domu nás seznámila. Snažil jsem se v rozhovoru, seč jsem byl, býti vlídným a roztomilým a zalíbit se onomu neznámému. Bavili jsme se dobře: bylo několik chvil srdečné veselosti, žertovného povídání a opravdové sdílnosti.

Konečně povstal onen pán a poroučel se.

Evening toilettes from the Anna Masáková fashion house, Elegantní Praha, January 1924, photograhp by F. Drtikol and Co.

CZECH FASHION

Its Creators and Producers ....

The new structure of the fashion industry in the Czech lands was developed during the 19th century. Over the course of time, fashion houses for men's and women's custom-made clothing were established. Already by the middle of the century, domestic producers, such as Robert Krach, Vendelín Mottl and others, had managed to assert themselves in the international market. Around 1880, they began to put company labels on their products. At the same time, ready-made garment production developed, concentrated primarily in the Moravian town of Prostějov. In style, the Czech tailoring firms oriented themselves to fashion originating in Vienna, where the most widely read fashion magazine, *Wiener Mode* — published in the Czech version as *Nové Pařížské Mody* — was also published.[18] Throughout the existence of the Habsburg monarchy there was lively migration of tailors and seamstresses between Vienna and the Czech lands. Czech tailors went to Vienna to gain experience and to improve their standard of living. Many returned home after a time, while the best settled in Vienna and contributed to the creation of Viennese fashion.

The situation changed substantially after 1918. The Austro-Hungarian monarchy ceased to exist, and the political and cultural orientation of the new Czechoslovak state shifted to France. Fashion, which for long had already had its natural center in Paris, was one of the areas where the turn towards France was most apparent. In the world of fashion, words like "France", "French", or "Paris" became a guarantee of quality and elegance. Magazines regularly published reports on Parisian fashion, and a number of Czech fashion magazines had their own correspondents in Paris. French appeared in the names of Czech fashion salons, such as Maison Chic, Madeleine, Maison Louvre. Fashion designs had French names. Even models presented at fashion shows bore French descriptions. Owners and designers of

large fashion houses twice-yearly travelled to Paris fashion shows, and training in Paris was the highest qualification for every tailor.

What then was the picture of Czech fashion created in such close connection with French styles? The expression that was most often used in reports on fashion, and on which the efforts of both craftsmen and artists were focused, was "elegance". The yearning for elegance did not only originate from the style of world fashion, but also from the ambition of the new Czech society to escape from provincialism and to be on a par with cultured European nations.[19] At the same time, in social circles which determined the contemporary taste, elegance was connected with the adjective "inconspicuousness". This characteristic of Czech fashion — inconspicuous elegance — is documented both by published fashion designs and museum collections of clothing in which we can hardly find ostentation, excesses, conspicuous ornamentation, or flashy colours.

Czech fashion was also practical. The considerable favour — next to the continually proclaimed French orientation of Czech fashion — was shown the practical English style as well as the choice of practical and unostentatious types of garments. Alternating trimming on collars and cuffs and entire sets of accessories — hat, shoes, gloves, belt — in diffrent variations of colour made the garments more elegant and interesting. Czech fashion had to follow economic conditions, which were stabilized after the First World War, but soon they were complicated again by the great economic crisis of the 1930s. However, Czech women were used to making up for limited financial resources with resourcefulness and their own skilfulness. In the inter-war period, fashion met the demands of the economic situation thanks to outfits combining various fabrics which called for a creative and practical approach toward fa-

Coat dress of grey gaberdine, Pražská moda, autumn–winter 1923 – 24

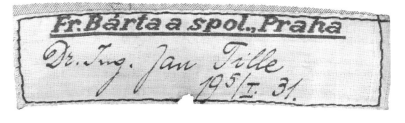

shion. The creation of these outfits was made easier by patterns that either appeared in magazines or were sent to readers by mail-order. The popularity of knitted jumpers, pullovers, vests, knitted dresses, bathing suits, and other parts of garments stimulated an interest in home-knitting, which was supported by various contests in women's magazines.

Czech fashion, as it appears in Czech fashion magazines, was also democratic and modest. More than with mondains, the young generation of female fashion journalists sympathized with modern girls and women from the less-wealthy middle classes, working women or mothers. Most of the fashion reports were directed towards such women: although they covered news of changes in fashion and styles of luxury clothing, they usually did this from the perspective of a modern practical woman and cautious Czech homemaker.

Foreigners' views of Czech women are also interesting to note. Maurice

Dress from the Arnoštka Roubíčková fashion house, photograph from 1923 – 24

Mosnier, director of the committee of international fairs in Paris, who organized a French fashion show at the Prague Sampling Fair in 1927, noted before the show that it was necessary to carefully select Parisian models because they would be subject to comparison, which could well be to their disadvantage. He considered Czechoslovak women to be perfectly built, with the lithe figures of ancient goddesses. Mr. Worth, who also visited Prague on the same occasion, expressed his deep respect for the good taste, distinction of manner, and restraint of Czech women in adopting the latest fashions. Worth was only sorry that care for the overall appearance, not only for clothing, was not as widespread in Czechoslovakia as it was in France. Finally, he claimed with French courtesy that Prague women were well on their way to

setting the tone in Central Europe, and thus to becoming second Parisians.[20]

Who created Czech fashion? The development of tailor production is documented by approximate statistics of Prague address books: while in 1910 there were 2, 980 tailors and 147 producers and merchants of ready-made clothing,[21] in 1924 we have records of 3, 640 tailors and 210 producers and merchants of ready-made clothing.[22] We can only gain a clear picture of a small number of these firms from advertisements published in magazines of the period, reports about their activities, photographs, and, in the case of several of them, from preserved artefacts. The picture of fashion production is completed by a number of companies producing women's and men's underwear (B. Mattula, Triola), more than 200 furriers (Penížek and Reiner, František Novotný), innumerable modistes (Máša Ehrlichová, Madame Tombo, Weill, Ella Reimannová, Zdeněk Rudolf), and hatmaking companies (Václav Čekan, Emil Wehle, Jan Weiss, Jaroslav Holub), glove-makers (Emil Engelmüller), bag and umbrella manufacturers. Thanks to Tomáš Baťa Czech shoes became famous the world over. Nevertheless, in every city local production of shoes flourished. The most famous shoemaking companies in Prague included Krása, Papež, Váňa, and others. The well-developed textile industry served fashion production, providing quality materials for mass consumption and domestic production of buttons, clasps, glass beads for embroidery, costume jewellery, and tailors' dummies.

Among the most famous and most luxurious women's fashion houses were those of Hana Podolská and Oldřich Rosenbaum, followed by those of Arnoštka Roubíčková, Elisa Ecksteinová, Anna Masáková, František Kotalík, Josefa Weigertová,

Franta Omcirk, Máša Ehrlichová, Klára Wasser-mannová, Štěpán Hoza, Zdenka Šubrtová, and later the salons called Mimi and Madelaine, and after 1938 by the fashion house of Heda Vlková and a number of others. In tailoring for men, the leading firms were those of František Bárta, Kníže, and Raimund Konečný. F. Matějovský, Vilém Kolář, the Grand atelier of Antonín Machalický, Josef Eiselt (sports clothing), and others sewed for both men and women.

From the very beginning of the Czechoslovak state, Prague tailors tried to create and develop a specific style of "Prague fashion". In 1922 the association Pražská móda was established. It had as its aim "the promotion of Prague fashion with regard to its practicality, good taste, and good quality". The association was supposed to design and publish original Prague fashion, to care for its legal protection, and to improve the taste and quality of both producers and consumers. Among the founding members of the association were the owners of hatmaking factories Josef Veider and Gustav Müller, the general secretary of the Chamber of Trade and Commerce JUDr. František Samek, the editors A. J. Beneš and Augusta Pachmayerová, Hana Podolská ("who with her wonderful husband can be considered the leader of Czech women's fashion houses...."), as well as Jarmila Kronbauerová, member of the National Theatre.[23]

Fashion production attained exceptional quality and development in Brno as well, where the traditional orientation towards Vienna after 1918 likewise shifted to Paris. Fashion in Brno was represented by the fashion houses "Femina" (E. Javůrková-Widhalmová), Maison Chic (Olga Schicková), as well as those of Mořic Hartmann, Mrs. Hällerová, Mrs. Vinařová, Mrs. Řehulová, and others.[24] As documented by garments found in Czech museums and collections, a number of fashion houses located in smaller Czech and Moravian towns were also well informed about fas-

hion tendencies, had tasteful and resourcefull designs of cuts, and were excellent tailors. Among them were the fashion houses of Matylda Holubová in Plzeň, F. Jarošová in Havlíčkův Brod, and Josef Plevka in Nové Benátky. The fashion house of Marie Presserová-Zolotarevová in Olomouc achieved exceptional quality. Between 1910 — 1920 it took inspiration from the Viennese artistic association Wiener Werkstätte on the basis of contacts local family Primavesi had with this association. The quality of Presserová-Zolotarevová's work from the 1930s can be compared with that of the best Prague firms.

Portrait of Zdeňka Fuchsová - Mayerová , around 1925

The salon of Arnoštka Roubíčková was one of the most famous and oldest fashion houses in Prague. It was founded on family tradition. Arnoštka's mother had already been a clothing merchant. The name of Arnoštka Roubíčková in 1910 appeared in a Prague address book as the owner of a tailoring firm for ladies in Prague II, Nekázanka 8.[25] At the beginning of the 1920s Arnoštka Roubíčková was listed in the address book as a tailor, and Ada and Helena Roubíčková

Wedding dress from the Rosenbaum fashion house, Elegantní Praha, October 1923, photograph by F. Drtikol and Co.

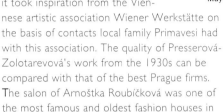

as draughtswomen, all of them at Wenceslaus Square 846/1, Prague II, ie. the Koruna palace.[26] We are well-informed of the appearance of this fashion house from the contemporary press, in which there appeared a reaction to criticism of working

Evening toilette from the Rosenbaum fashion house, Eva, March 1st, 1938, photograph by d'Ora, Paris

Jarmila Kronbauerová in the outfit
from the Podolská fashion house,
Elegantní Praha, May 1922

conditions of company employees. The fashion house had seven spacious workshops for tailors, two fur-processing rooms, one packaging and shipping room, two waterclosets for both men and women with wash rooms and proper ventilation.[27] In 1925 the owner of the firm had a fashion stage built on the first floor of the Koruna palace. It was a large hall with a stage made of precious woods in the middle, tables and armchairs for the audience in the corners, and display cases for fashion accessories between the columns on the sides of the hall. Dressing and changing rooms also were among the new facilities.[28]

The character of the work of the fashion house can be seen in designs by Ada Roubíčková, daughter of Arnoštka, which were regularly published in *Elegantní Praha*.

The Rosenbaum fashion house grew out of the firm of Eliška Rosenbaumová, who produced and sold ready-made garments for ladies at Štěpánská 53 in Prague II. Her name appears in Prague address books from 1907 and 1910. In the 1924-25 address book, the firm is listed among the tailor shops for ladies, with Oldřich Rosenbaum, son of Eliška, noted as owner. Rosenbaum was not satisfied

Fashion show in Chuchle, Eva, May 15th, 1933

with the firm's location in a side street, and so in 1928 he moved the firm to a new prestigious location, to a new building built in the functionalist style at Národní třída. He rented the two bottom floors, while the tailors' workshop of František Bárta occupied the upper floors. Within a short time an average firm producing ready-

made clothing was transformed into one of the most sought after and most luxurious fashion houses in Bohemia, whose customers were wives of Czech, German, and Jewish entrepreneurs from all Bohemia, actresses, wives of diplomats and other foreigners living in Prague, as well as a number of foreign clients that visited the firm from all over Europe. The firm was organized in the manner of French fashion houses: its director had the title of "directrice", and shop assistants were called "vendeuse". The quality of production was guaranteed by the fact that Rosenbaum employed highly-qualified workers, who complemented their knowledge of the tailor's craft with their own artistic ambitions. The "directrice" was Kristina Mayerová, who herself was trained as a tailor and had for many years worked in Vienna at the Grünbaum fashion house and at the Wiener Werkstätte.[31] The designer Berger also came from Wienna. He was later replaced by Niko Pauzder, a tailor and a painter. For a short time during the Spanish Civil War the Rosenbaum fashion house allegedly employed Cr. Balenciaga.[32] Sister-in-law of Kr. Mayerová, Zdeňka Fuchsová-Mayerová, worked also at the Rosenbaum fashion house as a draughtswoman and designer. She was a graduate of the School of Arts and Crafts in Prague and had attended course in painting at the Académie Collaris as well as a course for cutters (La femme de demain) in Paris, where she had also collaborated with *Jardin des Modes* magazine between 1931 and 1932. Besides her job at Rosenbaum, Fuchsová-Mayerová was also a permanent contributor to *Eva* and *Vkus* magazines, where she published her fashion designs and was active as a reporter during her stay in Paris.[33] Among others who contributed to the excellent reputation of the firm was František Vobecký, tailor, painter, photographer, and member of the Mánes artistic association. Oldřich Rosenbaum himself participated in the creation of the designs; he proved his artistic ta-

The Hana Podolská fashion
house in the Lucerna palace
in Prague, Český svět,
December 24, 1915

Portrait of Hedvika
Vlková , 1932

lent and imagination by creating his designs directly on models. Adina Mandlová, who worked at Rosenbaum as a model at the beginning of the 1930s, recalls that girls stood for long hours in the workshop while "Ulli" tried out his fantasies on them.[34]
The Rosenbaum salon operated like other luxury fashion houses in Prague: Rosenbaum and his designers traveled to Paris at least twice a year for the season and mid-season fashion shows. The photographic memory of Mrs. Fuchsová enabled her to sketch out the basic outlines of the models she had seen at fashion shows, at which sketching was strictly forbiden.[35] At the shows the Czech fashion houses always purchased several designs, which they then offered for sale to customers in Prague.
After fashion shows in Paris, Oldřich Rosenbaum and his designers travelled to the Riviera, where they worked out their inspirations from the shows and prepared their own collection. Collections were shown at least twice a year at fashion shows that took place directly in the Rosenbaum salon in Národní třída. They were open to invited guests only. Entrance was free and refreshments were served.[36] Oldřich Rosenbaum and Hana Podolská were the first to employ professional models. The Rosenbaum fashion house had a branch shop in Karlovy Vary and, according to an embroidered etiquette, also in Paris, although we have no other records regarding the Paris branch. In the 1930s, Rosenbaum collaborated with the Marthe Loeff company, which, like the Hana Podolská fashion house, was located in the building of the Riunione Adriatica Insurance company at Jungmannovo náměstí.

Both firms appeared in photographs taken at a fashion show that took place at the horseraces in Chuchle on May 7, 1933, under the joint-title "Rosenbaum-Marthe Loeff".
In addition to made-to-order garments, the Rosenbaum fashion house was also involved in making furs, which was world renowned.
According to Zdeňka Fuchsová, Doughlas Fairbanks and his wife were also clients of the firm.[37] Moreover Rosenbaum produced underwear, hats, and, after the model of French salons, also perfume. Oldřich Rosenbaum fled the German occupation of the Czech lands to the United States. His firm was sequestered and after 1948 was tranformed into the state-owned national clothing company "Styl". It continued its excellent tradition until 1992, when it ceased to exist.

Hilda Podolská , wife of Miloš Podolský
and a model in the Podolská fashion house,
photograph by Carola, 1938

The most important competitor of the Rosenbaum firm was the Hana Podolská fashion house. This firm was founded by the enterprising daughter of the architect Vošahlík. She helped to feed the family with work as a seamstress after her father died. When she married the painter Viktor Podolský, she set up a workshop with one seamstress.[38] Already in 1915 an advertisement and photograph of her newly opened elegant salon in the Lucerna palace appeared in *Český svět* magazine. Despite the tough competition of older and well-established tailoring firms, Hana Podolská managed to gain a large clientele among Czech actresses and ladies of high society. Between 1919 and 1924 Růžena Nasková, Jarmila Kronbauerová, Jarmila Novotná, and others allowed themselves to be photographed for magazines in garments by Podolská. Later clients included Olga Scheinpflugová, Eliška Junková, and Mrs. Hana Benešová. Podolská also sewed a number

Paul Poiret with Anny Ondráková and Parisian models in the film
"Únos bankéře Fuxe", Elegantní Praha, January 1924

**Portrait of Hana Podolská , photograph
by Carola, 1933**

of costumes for theatre productions and films, for example for the well-known Czech film comedy *Kristián*. In 1939 the Hana Podolská fashion house was awarded one of three top prizes at the international exhibition of crafts in Berlin.

The style of the fashion house was created by the owner herself together with the designer and draughtswoman Hedvika Vlková, who worked at Podolská from 1922 until 1938. Vlková was trained as a seamstress at the tailoring firm of Elisa Ecksteinová and in the tailors' association Maison Louvre in Prague. At the same time she attended courses in drawing at the Prague School of Arts and Crafts and the Academy of Fine Arts. She also combined artistic talent and her own artistic work with expert craftsmanship. Like Zdeňka Fuchsová, Heda Vlková was a long-time contributor to the fashion magazines *Eva* and *Vkus*, both as a draughtswoman as well as a Paris correspondent. František Vobecký came as a cutter to the Hana Podolská fashion house from the Rosenbaum company.[39]

The Hana Podolská (often written "Hanna") fashion house was the first Prague salon to pay close attention to advertising. Besides regular reports of Hana Podolská fashion shows, magazines also published photographs of the firm's designs presented by models, actresses, and women of high society, as well as photographs from the private life of the Podolská family, such as the wedding of Mrs. Podolská's son Viktor with Miss Věra Černá. Miss Černá was employed in the Hana Podolská fashion house as well as Podolská's two sons, Viktor and Miloš — the former as tailor and the latter as a furrier. Miloš's wife Hilda also worked for the fashion house as a model.

Besides tailoring, the Hana Podolská company was involved in fur working and hat making. The Hana Podolská fashion house survived the war years and was nationalized after 1948. It maintained the tradition and quality of the Hana Podolská company under the name Eva. It ceased to exist after 1989.

Hana Podolská was also one of the pioneers of a new form of presentation of fashion: fashion shows. They were preceded by fashion revues with unclear, confused, and often untasteful conception. In 1922, for example, a revue was criticized in which garments were presented as parts of scenes, taking place, for example, in bedrooms.[40] *Elegantní Praha* reported on a fashion show organized on the occasion of a car race at Zbraslav-Jíloviště, where the elegance of both the cars and their crews were judged. Thanks to a misunderstanding, the fashion show turned into a flower promenade.[41] Another curious example was an exhibition of the products of Vinohrady craftsmen that was combined with a fashion show. The show was relatively successful. "Tastefully and well-crafted designs were presented", but the models had to balance themselves among salamis, laden tables, and stone products.[42]

The Hana Podolská fashion show of December 1922 took place in the Hašek cabaret. Although it was only for invited guests, they managed to completely fill the hall and even formed a long line waiting in front of the cabaret. In December 1923, the Podolská fashion show took place in the Theatre of Comedy. At other times the shows took place in the firm's own display hall in the Lucerna palace. Although the latter site boasted a total of 300 seats, it still could not accommodate all guests.[43]

Fashion shows very quickly became common, regularly organized for example on the occasion of the Prague Sampling Fair. Mrs. Roubíčková or-

From the Podolská fashion house, Eva, March 15th, 1936

ganized two public fashion shows at the Prague Sampling Fair before 1924.[44] In September 1922 Antonín Machalický announced the establishment of a new tailoring company, "Grand Atelier" with the ambition to compete with the Parisian and English salons. As early as October he organized a fashion show which had to be repeated on the following day due to its great success.[45] From the following years we have reports of fashion shows of Anna Masáková, salon Rosenbaum, V. Kolář, F. Matějovský, K. Wassermannová, and Elisa Ecksteinová. Even a ready-made clothing company, Bon-ton, organized a fashion show in the display windows of its fashion house on Wenceslaus square.[46]

French fashion shows that took place in Prague served as a stimulus for Czech fashion creation. The first such show was that of Paul Poiret and took place in 1923. With his six mannequins, Poiret was at the same time involved in the shooting of a Czech film, "The Kidnap of Banker Fux". Despite rave reviews in the majority of publications, voices of criticism also appeared that pointed out that Paul Poiret already was not the best representative of French fashion.[47] Another French fashion show took place in 1927 on the occasion of the Prague Sampling Fair.[48] Original French designs from various salons were also presented at the shows of local fashion houses, as is evident for example from the advertisement of the Štěpán Hoza salon in 1934.[49]

Another type of garment producers were tailoring firms that, besides custom work, also produced ready-made garments in small series. One example is the Josefa Weigertová fashion house in Spálená street, which in its advertisement in *Modní revue* in 1927 explained to women the

advantages of both manners of acquiring clothing.[50] The František Friml firm presented itself in the similar way, even though in Prague address books the company, like many others, was listed as producing only ready-made clothing. Among such firms were listed fashion houses established already in the 19th century, like that of Josef Dědic, „Smíchovská dámská a dětská konfekce vlastní výroby Julie Eisnerová" (Smíchov Ladies' and Children's Ready-made Clothing Julie Eisnerová), „Konfekční závod U Černé Matky Boží Zdenka Malá" (Ready-made Clothing Firm at the Black Mother of the Lord Zdenka Malá), „Modní dům Schiller" (Fashion House Schiller), which also had a branch in Karlovy Vary, and others.

The Heda Vlková fashion house in Vodičkova street in Prague

Jiřina Šejbalová as Chloe in the play by John Galsworthy, dress from the Heda Vlková fashion house, photograph by Carola, Eva, May 15th, 1939

Large ready-made clothing firms had their factory outlets in Prague and other cities. The Rolný clothing factory in Prostějov sold its products in Prague, first in such department stores as "Novák" and „U města Paříže", and others, and later in a factory outlet it opened in the capital in 1922. According to Rolný statistics, immediately after the First World War, 10 % of the inhabitants of Czecho-slovakia purchased ready-made clothing; in 1935 the number was 75 %.[51]

Rolný produced men's, women's and children's ready-made clothes, as did another company from Prostějov, Nehera Co. Its owner, Jan Nehera, admitted in 1933 that in organizing the production and sales of his company he copied the methods of the shoe factory of Tomáš Baťa.[52] Large factories of ready-made clothing were also in Prague, where for example the Busch company, working mostly for export, encouraged women to select overcoats at its factory store by offering them factory prices.[53]

E. U.

Václav Čutta: Department store Novák, coloured litograph, printed by K. Kříž, Prague, around 1920, inv.no. GP 21193

Světlé kostymy pastelových barev zaplaví na jaře ulice. Nosí se s kabátkem otevřeným, odhalujícím bluzu, které věnuje móda velkou péči. Doplňují se stejnobarevným plstěným kloboukem a šálou v barvě bluzy nebo kostymu.

Summer outfits, drawing by V. Michal. Eva, April 1st, 1929

The Beginnings of Fashion Design and Drawing

Hedvika Vlková, Set of drawings of women's clothing, watercolour,
pencil-drawing, coloured with pastels, Prague, 1922 — 23

The Forms and Sources of INSPIRATION *of Czech Fashion*

From the beginning of the century, in Western fashion the job of „fashion creator" developed that was more involved in tailoring and style-development (French: „couturier") than the fashion designer, who had its historical predecessor in the draughtsman. Both creators and designers of fashion used above all drawings to communicate their ideas. In drawings the draughtsman or designer developed the models of the collection, which were then sewn and modeled on live mannequins. Throughout the season, drawings of the designs in the collection could be examined by customers in an album, which not only served to help them orient themselves in fashion, but also presented the individual designs that were available for order. The first such albums appeared in France in the 1880s. The draughtsman or designer was also an important element of communication between the client and the couturier, as he helped to refine the vision and to create the final form of the design that had been ordered. This is why in certain fashion houses the draughtsman complemented the couturier, who often lacked skill in drawing. Nevertheless, in the ideal case, the positions of designer and couturier could be filled by a single person.[54]

Interest in the publishing of garment designs grew with accelerating changes and development in fashion. The image of a model and fashion illustration of the draughtsman or designer became an unseparable part of not only a number of social and women's magazines, but also of the daily press. It gave rise to the establishment of even more specialized fashion magazines.

A more detailed profilation of Czech garment production, fashion, and its means and forms of distribution began in the period between 1918 and 1939. In fashion drawing, however, this lasted until 1948. This period of the history of Czech fashion placed emphasis on the work of the tailor-fashion creator (couturier), and gave birth to the designer (French „styliste") and with more demanding requirements on the work of the fashion draughtsman, working for the press, it also did the groundwork for fashion illustration.

Designers in Prague Fashion Houses

From 1922 until 1938, Hedvika Vlková (1901 — 1986) worked at the Hana Podolská fashion house as a draughtswoman and designer. Before her arrival, the job was filled by the husband of Mrs. Podolská, who was a painter. However, as Vlková later recalled, Mr. Podolský did this work irregularly and without pleasure.

How did the daughter of the garden architect Václav Vlk (1870 — 1964) and the domestic seamstress Marie, neé Fišerová (1871 — 1943), attain such a position in Prague? After graduating from the Higher School for Girls in Prague, Hedvika, the youngest daughter of the family, followed her mother's wish and learned to be a seamstress, while her two siblings studied at the university. Already within a short period working for Elsa Ecksteinová, Hedvika started designing clothes in addition to sewing them. Besides will and talent, she only had the love of drawing that she had had since childhood as well as the art classes at the Higher School for Girls. As her diary reveals, realizing that her future profession required higher artistic education, she decided to study while working. There was no special school for draughting in Prague, and so Hedvika began studying with the professor for ornamental drawing, A. Mudruňk,[55] and later with other professors. Finally, she decided to study full-time and became a student of the professor V. Nechleba, with whom she concentrated on

portraiture. She left the Academy of Fine Arts as an academic painter in 1931. In the same year, she received a stipend to Paris, where she worked at the Jacques Heim fashion house as a draughtswoman and in the evenings attended a course for cutters, La femme de demain. Vlková's work as draughtswoman and designer for the Podolská salon is documented in the Museum of Decorative Arts by a set of pencil drawings with coloured pastels of the format A5. The drawings include parts of the salon's collections from the mid 1920s and several older designs. A small part is made up of designs for individual clients. These drawings have the name of the customer written on the edge and also have pin holes, as it was customary to pin a piece of the fabric that was to be used for the garment to the design. Another set of drawings contains designs of Parisian fashion houses such as Chanel, Worth, Patou, and others (their names are given at the upper right-hand corner), which Vlková apparently drew upon returning from one of her first visits to Parisian fashion shows in the first half of the 1920s. As Vlková often recalled, drawing was strictly forbidden at fashion shows, and everywhere there were signs that said "Copier c'est voler!"

With the opening of her own fashion house Heda Vlková (1938 — 1949), this woman played an important role in the history of Czech fashion — this already in so far as she represented the owner-couturier and designer, giving appropriate supervision during execution of designs. She thus was able to make use of her training and experience as a seamstress and experience gained working at the Podolská fashion house. Because she did not have

her own fashion shows, she employed the otherwise normal means of presenting her own designs, depicting them in watercolours, examples of which are now in the possesion of the Museum of Decorative Arts in Prague.

Practically from the beginning of her career until the opening of her own business, Vlková also

Hedvika Vlková , Set of drawings of women's clothing, watercolour, Prague, 1925 — 26

sketched designs for the press. The advantage of the published designs lay in the fact that they revealed knowledge of the tailors' craft. They were executed with care for the logic of the cut and type of material. Cuts and details also reveal the ability to create something individual and executable.

As Vlková later often repeated,[56] her difficult course of training as designer had the effect that, in 1949, she undertook the task of founding, leading, and teaching, at first only a department and later an entire studio of fashion design, at the Academy of Applied Arts. She wanted to make it easier for others to follow the same path she had. From the beginning she placed emphasis on drawing and figural painting, drawing for design and publication, in addition to traditional techniques of design and finesses characteristic of la haute couture. Despite all the problems which education in fashion design faced in socialist Czechoslovakia especialy in the 1950s, one should note that training in drawing as an indivisible part of design was introduced in Parisian schools (such as Esmond), for example, not until 1970.[57] Like Mrs. Podolská in her fashion house, Rosenbaum had the final word in the creation of the style of his salon. In the words of Niko Pauzdr (born 1911, died in the 1980s), who worked at the fashion house as a draughtsman and a designer between 1930 and 1960, it was Mr. Rosenbaum who "decided on" the collection. Nevertheless, Zdeňka Fuchsová-Mayerová (1903 — 1988) played a similar role at the Rosenbaum fashion house between 1925 and 1937, as did Vlková at the Podolská salon. A student of the professors J. Krautová, E. Dítě, F. Kysela, and J. Mařatka at the Academy of Applied Arts, she roughly at the

same time attended courses in cutting and painting in Paris (Collaris). Vlková and Fuchsová-Mayerová knew each other, several times travelling together with their directrices to fashion shows in Paris. They had to hide the fact that they also met on other occasions because the secrecy of each fashion house was of the utmost importance. It was nevertheless known that the two fashion houses divided the orders from wealthy clients between themselves, since each concentrated on its own speciality: Podolská concentrated on costumes and overcoats, while Rosenbaum specialised in dresses, social outfits, and fur coats.

Both designers of the leading Prague fashion houses contributed their drawings to magazines. Hedvika Vlková contributed first to *Elegantní Praha*, *Agrární večerník*, and *Pražanka*, and later especially to the *Eva* magazine, from its first volume through 1938. Her drawings are calm, full of elegance and feminine subtlety, and with their considerably descriptive character they can be compared with the works of the French illustrator Pagés.

Hedvika Vlková , Spring outfits, Eva, March 1930

Zdeňka Fuchsová contributed to *Eva* with her considerably different style — flat, linear, and simple. However, her main work was done for Vkus (1934 — 1944). In contrast to Vlková, who later pursued her entrepreneurial and teaching career, Fuchsová concentrated on her work in design and illustration until the end of the 1950s.

Hedvika Vlková , Women's afternoon and less formal
evening dresses, watercolour, Paris, 1931

Ada Roubíčková , Designs for women's clothing, Elegantní Praha, May 1922

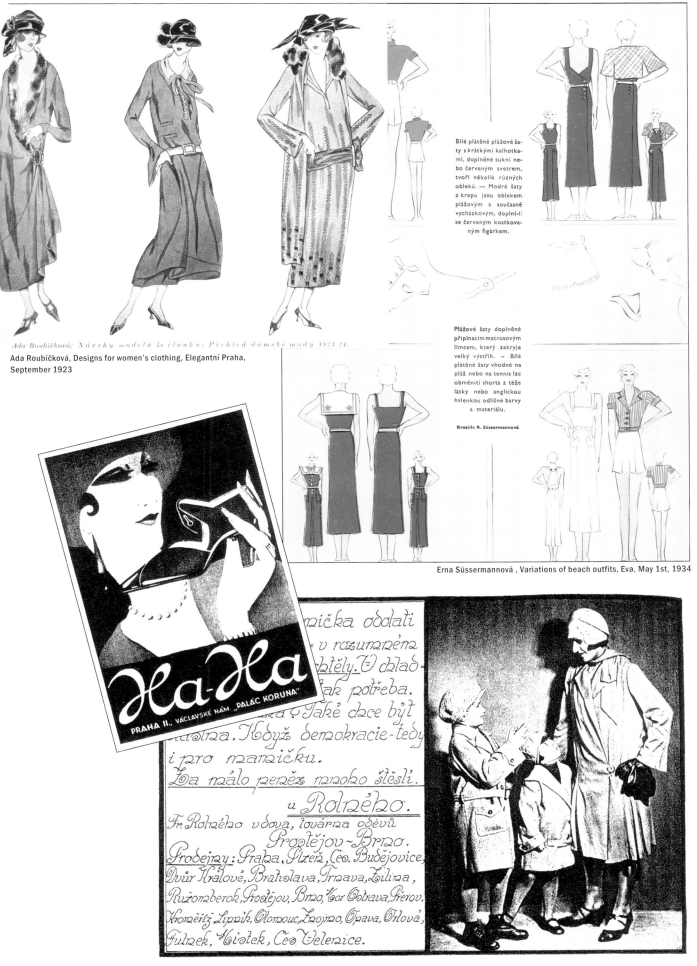

Ada Roubíčková: Návrhy modelů ke článku: Přehled dámské mody 1923-24.

Ada Roubíčková, Designs for women's clothing, Elegantní Praha, September 1923

Bílé plátěné plážové šaty s krátkými kalhotkami, doplněné sukní nebo červeným svetrem, tvoří několik různých obleků. — Modré šaty z krepu jsou oblekem plážovým a současně vycházkovým, doplní-li se červeným kostkovaným figárkem.

Plážové šaty doplněné připínacím matrosovým límcem, který zakryje velký výstřih. — Bílé plátěné šaty vhodné na pláž nebo na tennis lze obměniti shorts z téže látky nebo anglickou halenkou odlišné barvy a materiálu.

Kreslila R. Süssermannová

Erna Süssermannová , Variations of beach outfits, Eva, May 1st, 1934

Božena Vavrečková , Fashion drawing,
Měsíc, May 1932

Fashion drawing

A still-life from 1647 by the famous Czech engraver Václav Hollar,[58] depicting the gloves, muff, fur cape, and lace left behind by his model, is sometimes considered the forerunner of modern fashion drawing. It betrays the enchantement which many other painters have also come under before the beginning of the 20th century called for a specific genre of fashion illustration and drawing. René Bouché (1906 — 1963), a Czech emigrant [59] who worked and died in Paris, is coincidentally considered to be one of the greatest masters of this new genre. In contrast, the list of Czech fashion draughtsmen and illustrators working for the press — especially in the period 1918 to 1938 — is not very illustrious. Some of them lacked training in drawing, while others lacked sufficient courage. We do not find freer and more expressive illustrations in the Czech press until the 1940s.[60] Czech fashion drawing of the 20th century really began to develop in *Elegantní Praha*, which appeared between 1922 — 1925.[61]

Hedvika Vlková contributed several watercolour figures to this magazine. The style of Ada Roubíčková, daughter of the owner of the Prague salon Arnoštka Roubíčková, was surer in its execution. The younger Roubíčková studied fashion drawing in Vienna. Another contributor to the magazine, Erna Süssermannová-Veselá-Volavková, trained in Berlin, taught fashion and model drawing in the Rotter advertising agency located in Vodičkova street in the U Nováků building.[62] Fashion draughtswomen, often only skilfull copiers who copied and partially modified designs from magazines and then offered them for sale to home sewers, allegedly were trained at such short-term courses.[63]

Pavla Pitchová contributed her well-executed double page drawings and at times smaller sketches to *Salon magazine* (1922 — 1931), a "revue for fashion, society, art, and pleasant things in life" that was a high-class magazine in large format. Her typical initials PP appeared in other magazines and newspapers, though not so well-drawn and graphically designed. Her drawings evoke more than they design fashion.

The free, expressive illustrations of Božena Vavrečková belong to the few drawings that distinguish themselves in quality from the linear, rather flat drawings that were generally more common. We know that she, too, received her art training in Vienna during her stay there with her diplomat father. In the first half of the 1930s, her drawings appeared several times in *Měsíc* magazine (1932 — 1939), published in Brno, and in *Eva*. The painter Vojtěch Michal also began contributing his linear drawings to *Eva* in the 1930s.

Pražská moda (1923 — 49), which was published by the Prague association of tailors of the same name, was strictly devoted to fashion. Drawings made in various techniques were executed by Prague artists and painters.[64] *Pražská moda* was in fact an album of separate fashion sheets and was published quarterly. It has great documentary value for the development especially of men's fashion. At the same time, it presented a unique kind of drawing which was supposed to serve as an aid to clients' imagination and to tailors, who sewed according to it. The magazine's slightly conservative style was expressed in its slick and hyper-realistic appearance, which was also applied to the figure and face of elegant gentlemen and, in some cases, sportsmen. The magazine offered Czech men a model not only for clothing, but also for elegant appearance, attitude, gesture, and perhaps also behaviour. The figure in this older type of fashion drawing was of secondary importance and thus was often unlively.

Non-Fashion Sources of Czech Design

To only describe the work of experienced designers of fashion houses, tailors, and illustrators of fashion magazines and newspaper columns would restrict and impoverish our understanding of the development of individual images of garments and their styles. The desire, need, and courage of numerous women and men to design outfits according to their own taste was first in evidence in the second half of the 19th century. Their efforts undoubtedly increased in the 20th century together not only with the liberation of clothing from social chains and meaning, but also with the new role of women's individuality and uniqueness. This process was undoubtedly further emphasized by the over-authoritative dictates of fashion styles and the majority of articles in fashion magazines that wrote with naive admiration and a certain narrow-mindedness about fashion tendencies and their particulars. There was also an incongruence between Western styles of fashion and the Czechoslovak social and climatic conditions, as well as between the Czechoslovak female figure and, for example, petit French women. Nevertheless, the aesthetic appeal of modern architecture and applied art seems to have been of relatively greater importance.

In their publicistic activity, both Staša Jílovská and Milena Jesenská drew attention to the changed conditions of life, material culture, and individuality of women. Jesenská in particular wrote very eloquently in this spirit. Even the titles of the two collections of Jesenská's newspaper articles (*Člověk dělá šaty, Cesta k jednoduchosti — A Person Makes Clothes, Path to Simplicity*), which were published in book form in the middle of the 1920s, reveal her much different understanding of contemporary women's clothing. Milena Jesenská contributed an article with the striking title, *Mají svobodnou vůli, ale šatů nemají* (*They have free will, but no clothes*) to the bi-lingual publication *Civilisovaná Žena — Zivilisierte Frau* (*Civilized Woman*, Brno, 1929 — 30), which accompanied the exhibition of the same name organized by J. Vaněk (1891 — 1962) and Z. Rossmann. The two men were, together with Božena Horneková (later Rothmayerová, 1899 — 1984), the authors of the publication. The publication *Civilized Woman* (94 pages) was very critical of contemporary fashion which, according to its authors,

turned from the previous simplicity to unnecessary complexity. Its subtitle was „How should the cultivated woman dress?" Božena Horneková, a textile designer, teacher, and graduate from Academy of Applied Arts (1915 — 1921), gave answer. The book contained a new conception of women's garments based not on skirts but strictly on trousers: long, straight, wide in such a way that they formed the outline of a skirt, as well as trousers reaching below the knees resembling golf trousers. The majority of these trousers reached the waist, while work and maternity trousers had the form of overalls with braces and in some cases a sleeveless bodice. Depending on whether they were for work, for school, or the job (typical professions are depicted), for the home, for bed, or for social occasions, they were of various materials and colours, complemented by shirt blouses, vests, jackets, as well as, in winter, by overcoats, and, at home, by morning robes. To Horneková, even corpulent women looked better in trousers, as did pregnant women — a notion that was at the time still quite revolutionary. The new style of garments also required

Pavla Pitschová , Travelling outfits, Salon, June 1929

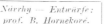

Návrhy — Entwürfe: prof. B. Hornekové.

87

Božena Horneková , Designs for women's trouser suits, Civilisovaná žena, Brno 1929

a certain kind of underwear and a rational approach to dressing. Even accessories were not left to chance. *Civilisovaná žena* contained absolutely all kinds of garments and accessories. We do not know whether all of the exhibited garments and accessories were in fact executed in real size and material and displayed at the exhibition to complement the modern home interiors and kitchens with electric appliances to which the exhibition was dedicated.[65] Only such garments could form a coherent part of modern architecture and design. Other, fashionable garments could in no way serve this function.

The painter Josef Čapek was one of the few who reacted to this brash change of wardrobe of contemporary women when, in an article in *Lidové noviny* from March 1930, he reproached the "designers" for drawing inspiration from men's clothing, which Čapek admitted had many insufficiencies.[66] However, Horneková created with her trouser outfits a new clothing style that responded to the image of a woman — "free", as Jesenská often wrote, sporty, fresh, practical, rather more boyish than feminine, more a student of life or intellectual than a mother, lady, or coquette.

Horneková's drawings were instructive and descriptive, without greater artistic ambitions, because they represented a new concept of clothing. They resembled more work done in school on a given theme than designs or even fashion drawings. Despite this, they were important not only for Czech, but also for European garment creation. They were at least forty years before their time, as girls and women did not commonly wear such clothing at work and socially until the 1970s. At the turn of the 1920s and 1930s, and particularly in Central Europe, trousers were of course considered to be fashionable, and therefore only a passing fad. Let us also devote attention to other drawn designs, some of which were also executed — to those designs which drew their inspiration from folk traditions of clothing and decoration like embroidery and lace-work. For example, in the fashion column of *Ženské listy* from the years 1915 — 1917, we can find a number of designs of "folkloristic", "Czech", or simply "our" fashion. In opposition to Western fashion styles, these designs declared themselves to be "clothing that was practical, thoughtful, "artistic", and "dignified enough for today's woman" (as stressed by the

were presented as appropriate for the summer, for stays in the countryside, as well as for children and girls.[68] At the same time, we should not forget that original folk dress could still commonly be seen throughout the first half of the 20th century in Moravia, Slovakia, and in many parts of Bohemia. Striking features of this clothing offered possible application and created an unforgettable impression on foreigners.

íno,
äh,

v kanceláři, v obchodě,
in der Kanzlei, im Geschäft,

ve škole,
in der Schule,

The article by Nicolace Bonnechos in *Gazette du Bon Ton* from June 1920, confirms this. The article is accompanied by an example of "Czechoslovak fashion" as it was understood by one of the participants of a delegation that visited the young Czechoslovakia at that time. The garment design called "Mrtvý ptáček" (Dead Little Bird) betrayed its inspiration from the richly folded sleeves of local folk dresses and richly embroidered men's vests.[69] At the end of the article, N. Bonnechos expressed exceptional admiration for the folk dress and unconsciously expressed what "our" fashion also wanted: "And so face to face with these enchanting folk costumes, serious and often at the same time gay, we became ashamed of our straight jackets and trousers lacking any style. We wanted some painter to capture a few examples of these beautiful garments, whose decorative elements could so easily be used to revive our Western fashion."

L'OISEAU MORT

**Gazette du Bon Ton,
June 1920**

Starting in the 1960s, folklore and ethnic styles became common elements in European fashion. As far as their future is concerned, it seems bright.

H. J.

o večer, domácí
vnosti, divadlo,
r den Abend,
usfeste und Theater,

Na cesty.
Auf Reisen.

Na cesty.
Auf Reisen.

authour of the article, R. Tollnerová). Until then, fashion inspired by folklore had been considered to be worn for baser political and patriotic reasons, and was thought to be aesthetically unattractive and an anachronism.[67] Today, however, we should regard them as certain attempts to develop an original form of clothing, as yet another possibility for dressing that coexisted with fashionable dress and often even was based on it. In the period in question, many of the distinctive designs

PHOTOGRAPHY
and fashion
in the Intermezzo
OF THE TWO WORLD WARS

Fashion photography has a history as long as photography in general. A visit to a photographer's studio was always a special occasion, and a fashionable dress or suit belonged to it without exception. The resulting work usually had the form of a formal portrait. Already in the last century, photographs were put into family albums or, in the case of important personalities, were also sold as interior decorations. Already before the First World War, the outstanding Prague photographic studios, such as that of F. J. Langhans, V. J. Bufka, J. Posselt, Wild, Manger, Schlosser and Wenisch, Vaněk and Kanderál, later also Balzar, and others, were able to meet even the most demanding requests of their customers.

In the 1890s, so-called snapshots began to be widely used in the social life sections of magazines, such as *Světozor* and, after 1904, *Český svět*. The unsurpassed master of instantaneous photography was R. Bruner-Dvořák. Shots of hunts, horseraces, and other events were the most convincing evidence of the lifestyle and fashion trends of social and cultural celebrities.[70]

A special position was held by F. Drtikol & Co., located in Vodičkova street. Already in the pre-war period, the firm worked with the specialized magazine *Elegantní svět*. Published photographs were created in the style of the fading Art Nouveau. In such photographs, perfect portrait studio work melded with the need to provide information about new clothing designs. The photographs were usually of ladies of high-society, theatre and also film actresses. The photographs were complemented by written information about the identity of the person and the fashion houses that had provided the garments. Both the individuality and elegance of the photographed person and the dress itself was valued. The ideal was a harmony of both elements.

Fr. Drtikol,
Portrait, 1923,
carbon-process

After the foundation of the independent Czechoslovak Republic, photography began to become part of fashion advertising more than ever. The dominant position was still held by the F. Drtikol & Co. studio, which especially in the 1920s provided photographs to some of the newly founded magazines concerned more or less with fashion and lifestyle. These were, above all, *Moda a vkus*, *Salon*, *Gentleman*, *Elegantní Praha*, and later *Eva*. The extravagance and exclusivity of the dresses was in accord with Drtikol's interpretation of a woman as a self-confident and dynamic personality with an unconcealed erotic spirit. This impression was further enhanced by the fact that the models were mostly dark-haired, dressed in dark clothes, and were photographed against dark backgrounds. Most often Drtikol collaborated with the fashion house of Hanna Podolská and A. Masáková at Královské Vinohrady in Prague.[71]

Often published were also photographs of the leading Parisian photographic studio, Madame d'Ora, whose owner, Dora Kallmus, had worked in Karlovy Vary in the first half of the 1920s. This was exclusive information, in photographic form, straight from the fashion capital of Paris. The photographer later commented on her own work: "My interest in portraits remained with me in fashion — I prefer photographs of the upper part of the body, and most of all, I like to

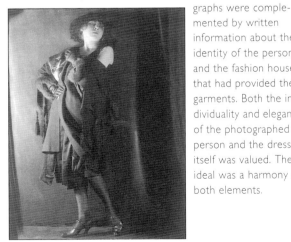

Fr. Drtikol, Portrait study, 1922, carbon-process

Fr. Drtikol, Portrait study, 1925, bromide-process

take pictures of hats, blouses, and wrappers. This also applies to formal and sporty garments. As far as full figures are concerned, I most like to photograph stylish toilettes with wide folded skirts. The most pleasant thing for me is to take a picture of a beautiful face, complemented by a hat, collar, and framed by a haircut".[72] In the 1930s, a similar method was employed by some Prague photographic firms, of which the Carola studio was the most popular and extensive in its production.

The magazine *Pestrý týden* began to be published in 1926. It was conceptually based on photographs that documented current events at home and abroad. The magazine's unceasing demand for new photographic material was later filled by a generation of photographers that shot pictures especially for the press. The key personality here was K. Hájek. Next to him, working especially outside the studio, were V. Jírů, J. Lukas, S. Štochl, and others. B. Šťastný managed to

a much wider spectrum of society. The most important advertising photographer in Prague was J. Sudek, who collaborated especially with the publishing house Družstevní práce and with "the picture magazine of today", *Žijeme* 1930 of the Union of Czechoslovak Artwork. However, Sudek did not focus on fashion photography. We only know of his collaboration with the shoemaking firms of Popper and GEC. The photographs of hygienic children's clothing, as advertised by the Red Cross, were published in book form. A special position was held by the younger F. Vobecký. After a study trip to Paris between 1926 and 1927, where he studied painting at several private schools, Vobecký worked in the leading Prague fashion houses Rosenbaum and Podolská as a cutter and designer. At the same time he was active as both a painter and photographer. In addition to being a member of the Mánes artistic association, through which he exhibited his paintings and photographs, he published fashion photographs in *Měsíc* magazine starting in 1932.

The ever greater demand for new advertising and promotional specialists in the inter-war period was filled by several specialized institutions. These were the School of Arts and Crafts in Bratislava, the School of Arts and Crafts in Brno, and the Prague State School of Graphic Art. Important were contacts with the avantgarde Bauhaus movement, in whose spirit the education was conducted in the 1930s. Of a number of important teachers, we should mention at least J. Funke, E. Hrbek, J. Ehm, and Z. Rossmann, who educated many successful advertising photographers.

Fr. Drtikol, Photograph of fashion, 1924, bromide-process

work as a magazine photographer and at the same time as a studio photographer creating fashion photographs. This is documented by advertisements for the furs of the Novotný company or the goods of the Papež shoemaking firm. The beginning of the 1930s and the deep economic crisis brought them a change in advertising strategies. Fashion photographs began to be used more for general promotion of ready-made and large-scale production, which appealed to

The work of F. Kollár developed in Paris outside
the framework of Czech and Slovak photography. Between 1932 and 1948 he collaborated
with the Parisian branch of *Harper's Bazaar* and
many other French and German fashion magazines. He ranks among the most significant personalities of fashion photography. In recent
years his work has been at the center of exhibition and publishing interest in France.[73]

An exceptional position in the clothing industry
between the two world wars belonged to the
shoemaking and rubbermaking company of Tomáš Baťa in Zlín. The company had its own advertising and promotional department. In 1933,
P. Hrdlička, a graduate of the State School of
Graphic Arts in Prague, was hired as the first
promotional photographer of the company. At
that time, the department had more than sixty
employees who worked on promotional materials for season collections and other campaigns.
For example, every week the promotional elements for display windows of the network of
Baťa shops throughout the whole country were
designed, produced, and distributed. In addition
to the work of a number of graphic artists and
text composers, photography became a part
of the company's promotional materials.

In the middle of the 1930s, already under the
management of Jan Baťa, the firm set up its own
film studios to produce promotional and documentary films. Involved in their beginnings were
L. Kolda (production), E. Klos and K. Plicka (direction), P. Hrdlička and J. Lukas (camera), A.
Hackenschmied (cut), and many other personalities of the photographic and film world. The
promotion of the firm's products and fashion
trends with the help of the most modern methods of mass communication reached a higher
level.

J. M.

Emil Weiss: Šlemr shoes. Prague 1926
coloured lithograph. Printed by Průmyslová
tiskárna, Praha VII, inv. no. GP 10566

Vilém Rotter: Sport coats Praga.
Coloured lithograph,
printed by B. Hora, Prague 1930
inv.no.GP 10522

ADVERTISING

in the Czechoslovak First Republic

After the First World War and the foundation of the independent state of Czechoslovakia, advertising adopted the patriotic tone of a certain neo-classicism with elements of folklore and the requisite national colours of white, red, and blue. The influence of Czech Cubism also at times appeared. Roughly in the first third of the 1920s, a certain link to contemporary European artistic currents was in evidence, possibly also stimulated by several exhibitions of advertising and posters from France. The years 1925 to 1930 can be considered as the last heyday of beautiful posters, which were at this time still the most important media for advertising. Large, full-page advertisements in magazines continued for a long time to be black-and-white, and furthermore were often but smaller versions of posters.

Posters were undoubtedly influenced by the new decorativism (later called Art Deco after the exhibition of the same name in Paris in 1925), with which a part of "national decorativism" easily melded. Posters, though they were aesthetically the most pleasing, nevertheless made up only a small part of the production of these years. The great majority of advertisements were dry, factual posters, lacking not only the lightness and elegance of Art Deco, but often also the humour of posters of the pre-war period and before.

Höns: Outfits BAYER. Coloured lithograph. Printed by Průmyslová tiskárna, Prague 1927, inv.no. GP 20241

A characteristic feature of advertising in the 1920s and 1930s was the almost absolute hegemony of professionals from advertising studios, agencies, and offices, who effectively prevented amateurs from working in the industry. Advertising became independent, an almost scientifically managed business. The designer was only one member of a whole team of employees of such agencies, in fact more an executor rather than initiator. The most influential and powerful agencies and studios (PIRAS, Pacold, UR-Praga, Richter, Estra, Remo, Hofbauer-Pokorný, Dec Art, Rax, AUR, Rotter, and others) employed, either directly or on commission, tens of artists, of whom we should mention at least Emil Weiss, Leo Heilbrunn, Zdeněk Rykr, Jiří Jelínek, Höns, Hanns Jakesch, and Josef Čejka. An especially characteristic feature of the 1920s was the variety of work of individual artists, studios, and agencies. It is not unusual to see works that are at times in the style of Art Deco, at others rather dry and factual, and other posters that are more humorous, all by the same artist.

A second specific characteristic of advertising in the 1920s and 1930s is the establishment by firms of their own advertising departments. A pioneer in this was evidently the Schicht company in Ústí nad Labem and the Waldes company in Prague, soon followed by others, such as Baťa and Nehera in fashion, and international Elida in cosmetics.

At the end of the 1920s, the new functionalist typography and photography took over in advertising. Examples of the quick shift to avant garde design are the relatively minute posters of two "women's" exhibitions in Brno in 1929.

Vilém Rotter: Tenis outfits „Praga" from the factory. Coloured lithograph,
printed by Lito B. Hora, Prague 1930, inv.no. GP 10502

Milén's poster for the Exhibition of the Modern
Woman has the new typography still with a drawing of a woman's Art Deco head, while
Rossman's poster for the *Civilized Woman* exhibition employed, besides functional typography,
only a photograph of a woman's head with a
long braid unmercifully being cut with scissors.
The 1930s witnessed the definitive victory of
modernism and strict practicality. The elegant
and slightly frivolous woman of Art Deco posters of the 1920s disappeared and was replaced
by abstracted silhouettes, figures, or, in the best
case, hyper-realistic, sometimes even "pop" drawings.

Decisive were crisp, bright colours over large
surfaces, large formats (the walls of entire buil-
dings appeared covered with advertisements),
striking lettering expressing the text in a single
slogan, often a single word that could be easily
remembered by the subconscious. Sometimes
only the logo of a large company sufficed.

Höns: Fabrics Prokop a Čáp. Coloured lithograph,
printed by V. Neubert and So., Prague 1927, inv.no. GP 20362

Fashion Advertising

A number of artistically interesting posters that
are rich in ideas have been preserved from the
1920s and 1930s, designed especially by experienced professionals working for various clients.
In the 1920s, some of these artists (including
Gemka, Heilbrunn, Höns, Jakesch, Smatek,
K. Weiss, Pacold studio, PIRAS, Ra, and others)
were able to move between decorativism on
the one hand, and objectivity on the other.
Some of their posters, such as Jakesch's advertisement for Bruna shoes; Weiss' posters for the
Elite, Kříž, Löbl, and Šlemr companies; Höns'
work for Bayer, Prokop, and Čáp; or posters by
an unknown artist for Papež shoes, can be favo-
rably compared with the best French and English
work in these years.

In the 1930s, new studios and designers appeared on the scene, including Grygar, Gub's studio
UR-Praga, Flenyk's AUR, Hofbauer-Pokorný,
Jonáš, the previously mentioned Rotter,
Wartusch, and others, whose bold modernist
production pushed aside the elegance of the
1920s.

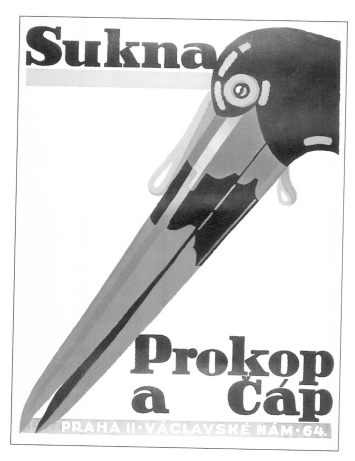

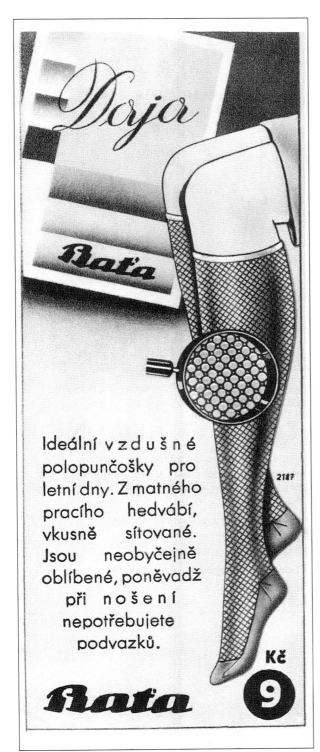

Fashion, or, better said, the contemporary lifestyle of which fashion is a part, was also promoted by advertising for perfumes, cosmetics, tobacco products, jewelry, cars, sport equipment, cafes, entertainment establishments, magazines, department stores, as well as promotion of spas and tourist centers, various services, etc. The contemporary lifestyle was also presented with incredible success in hundreds of West European, American, and Czech films, often featuring famous movie stars, which were shown in dozens of cinemas in both the center and outskirts of Prague, as well as in smaller towns and villages throughout the country. Fashion could also be seen in dozens of melodramas by contemporary writers staged by boulevard theatres in the center of Prague, as well as in epic revues of less important theatres. Fashion was advertised both by special fashion magazines and social magazines of general interests, like *Salon*, *Světozor*, and *Pestrý týden*. At the beginning of the 1930s, the drawings by the graphic designers of these magazines, such as J. Jelínek, S. Rotterová, L. Lepařová, P. Pitschová, and L. Ruppová, were complemented and gradually replaced by photographs of fashion designs of various salons taken by Drtikol, Schlosser and Wenisch, and other photographic studios. Some photographs were also acquired from foreign photographic studios, such as the international d'Ora company. In the 1930s there appeared, particularly on the covers of fashion revues, modernist montages combining photographs with drawings.

Posters of fashion houses like Podolská have not been preserved, in part perhaps because modest advertisement in revues and magazines was sufficient for such high-class firms. Mass street advertising was primarily the work of large-scale producers.

The major theme of advertising always — including during the First Republic — has been the woman: usually elegant, seductive, unattainable, and at the same time available. Only the „sporty" end of the 1920s and beginning of the 1930s introduced an occasional man into advertising. He was, nevertheless, seldom alone, most often accompanied by a woman.

P. Š.

Fashion Magazines & Fashion Journalism

In the period between the two world wars, fashion journalism was very widespread in the Czech lands. Besides specifically fashion magazines, there were a number of magazines of general interest in which a significant part was devoted to fashion, as well as specialized professional publications and fashion columns in the larger daily newspapers.

Fashion magazines were meant for amateur readers, seamstresses, and tailors. Some of these publications had already been founded several decades earlier as Czech versions of foreign magazines. Among these were the German *Bazar* or *Nové Pařížské Mody*, which was the Czech version of the Viennese *Wiener Mode*. In the time of the First Republic, these publications reprinted foreign fashion illustrations, but their contents were gradually reoriented to the Czech environment. The magazine *Modní svět*, published in Mladá Boleslav from 1879 as a reprint of the German *Modenwelt*, changed its name to *Lada-Modní Svět* with the subtitle "Weekly of Intelligent Women". Under the editorship of Olga Vojáčková, it became a magazine of general interest. Starting in 1921, the magazine *Pařížský Vkus* began to be published by Jaroslav Burian in Písek. Although the magazine presented itself as a Czech publication with main offices in Paris, it was published by the Bachwitz fashion studio in Vienna as a translation of the *Chic Parisienne* magazine. *Pražská módní přehlídka (Prague Fashion Review)*, published between 1924 and 1925, was of the same origin. The magazine published models with French texts, translated into Czech in supplement. Karel Ločák and Libuše Žižková served on the editorial staff of *Česká móda* until 1932. The creation of the Czech magazine *Moda a vkus*, which pro-

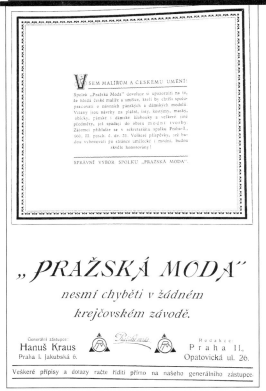

Pražská moda, Prague 1923

claimed itself for world fashion, was an important event in the Czech fashion world. Though it tended to favour French fashion, it juxtaposed this with American fashion, which it recommended to Czech women for its practicality and restraint. The editor Olga Fastrová managed to gather a group of fashion designers on the editing staff who were mostly graduates from the Prague School of Arts and Crafts, including Marie Fischerová-Kvěchová, Hana Dostálová, Zdena Liebscherová-Čechová, Anna Lukášová and Tyda Malcová. They all worked together with the Parisian designer M. Giblet and the Czech draughtsman Rigo Schönborn, who previously worked in Paris. Olga Fastrová, born in 1876 in Prague, ranked among the most experienced Czech journalists concentrating on fashion and women's problems in general. Originally a teacher, upon marrying the writer Otto Fastr, she became involved in publishing and editing *Divadelní listy* magazine. After 1907, when she became

Dámské Modní Listy, Prague 192

Moda a vkus, drawing
by M. Giblet, Prague
1919

a widow, she earned living for herself and her three daughters with translations, her own literary works, and as a publicist. Under the pseudonym "Yvonna" she published her well-informed fashion reports in *Národní politika* in the period before the First World War.[74]

Another group of publications consisted of fashion magazines published for professionals — tailors and seamstresses. *Dámské Modní Listy* were published from the beginning of the 20th century until 1924. Between 1899 and 1943 Jan and Václav Kratina published *Dámské Akademické Modní Listy* as an organ of the "*První modní akademie Pražská ku pěstování mod a umění střihačského*" (The First Prague Fashion Academy for Fashion and Cutting Art). The magazine published French designs and had its parallel publication for males in *Akademické Modní Listy*, later called *Grand Mode Album*, published by the same house between 1898 and 1934. Besides designs and cuts, the magazine also contained elaborate technical descriptions for making garments.

Pražská moda was published between 1923 and 1949 by an association of Prague tailors of the same name, established in 1922. Among the editors were A. J. Beneš, Gustav Müller and Augusta

Pařížský vkus 1925

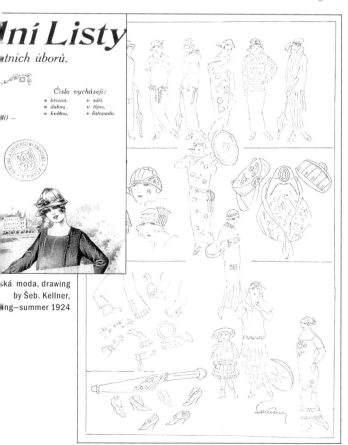

ká moda, drawing
by Šeb. Kellner,
ng—summer 1924

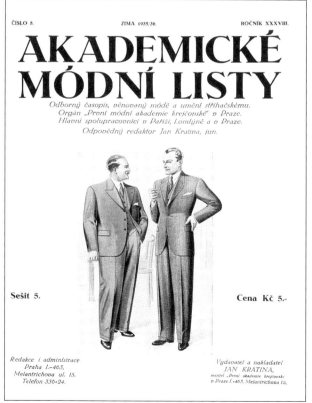

Akademické Módní Listy, Prague, winter 1935/36

Pachmayerová, who was a very active fashion journalist who published her articles in the *Český svéráz* magazine, *Modní revue*, and later also in *Měsíc*. Numerous Prague fashion specialists contributed to the publishing of *Pražská moda*. The magazine published original designs of women's and also men's clothing together with the names of designers. Among the designers were such personalities as Šebestián Kellner, a graduate from the Viennese and Prague Academy of Fine Arts, an illustrator and portrait painter, and the painter Ludmila Melková-Ondrušová, a graduate from the School of Arts and Crafts and the Academy of Fine Arts in Prague.

Vkus magazine, published between 1934 and 1944 by the Melantrich publishing house, was focused on practical issues. It was edited by Marie Rojíková and produced in collaboration with designers who concurrently worked for the *Eva* magazine. Most published models were complemented by matching cuts available for

Elegantn í Praha, cover by Rigo Schönborn, June 1922

order so that the design could be made at home. There also existed numerous specialised magazines. Every kind of textile production and fashion design had its own magazine — producers of ready-made clothing, cutters, tailors, tailors' assistants, hatmakers, modistes, glovemakers, shoemakers, merchants, employees of the knitting and weaving industry, and other professionals. In many kinds of professions there existed separate Czech and German magazines. Some magazines also had various political orientations. Besides these specialized publications, there were also company magazines, which provided information on events within the factory, successes in production and sales, but also on new fashion developments. Among the best such publications was *Dobrý odbyt* of the Sochor textile factory in Dvůr Králové, edited by Pavla Lindová-Gutfreundová, or *Magazin Rolný*, published by the Rolný ready-made clothing factory in Prostějov. Another Prostějov magazine, *Naše služba — zprávy firmy Nehera*, maintained a high professional and educational level. Its first editor was Zdenka Wolkerová, who was with the magazine from June 1st, 1933.

Specific products of the period, whose purpose went far beyond the world of fashion, were social magazines providing information on society, litera-

Elegantní Praha, cover by Rigo Schönborn, October 1922

egantní Praha, cover, Christmas 1923

cutive editor was the architect Josef Svoboda, and among the editors of the art section were the fashion designer Ada Rou-bíčková, Raimund Konečný jr., and Rigo Schön-born. Josef Šíma worked as the magazine's Paris correspondent. Among the members of the board of editors were leading Prague fashion houses, such as Marie Hulpachová, Vilém Kolář, Raimund Konečný, Anna Masáková, František Matějovský, Hana Podolská, Rosenbaum, and Arnoštka Roubíčková. Inda Navrátilová, Ada Roubíčková, Hana Podolská, R. Konečný, and F. Matějovský published in *Elegantní Praha* their fashion articles and reports from fashion shows both in Paris and Czechoslovakia.

Salon magazine, published from 1922, provided information on art, literature, sport, and social life. It contained fashion reports and practical advice on tasteful clothing. It was written by Olga Vojáčková and complemented by the drawings of Pavla Pitschová.

Gentleman, published between the years 1924 and 1929, was a men's revue for "men who aim for perfection in their appearance as well as in their acts and behaviour". It helped to create the ideal of the "progressive man, which means one who is self-educating, noble in soul, physically fit, of steady and unselfish character, with a reasonable and also happy life — simply put, a modern man".[76]

One section of the magazine regularly focused on fashion. It was written by Josef Eiselt, the-owner of a fashion house concentrating on sport outfits. The section provided good information on the etiquette of men's clothing, and new styles in cuts and materials. It was predominantly oriented toward English fashion.

The illustrated review *Měsíc*, published by Dr. Bohuš Kilian and the architect Václav Roštlapil in Prague and Brno from 1932, accustomed readers especially to contemporary art and architecture. Women's fashion was considered to be a part of lifestyle, and it was covered with fashion reports by Míla Tilschová, which were complemented with drawings by Božena Vavrečková, who later married the builder Václav Havel, and photographs of designs from Brno and Prague fashion houses.

The first issue of *Eva — Časopis vzdělané ženy*

ture, art, music, sport, etc., all with a somewhat educational intention.[75] One of the first such magazines was *Elegantní Praha,* published between the years 1922 and 1925. Its aim was to provide Czechoslovak and foreign intelligentsia with information about "the way the young republic is walking", about Czech culture, art, and industry, and at the same time to contribute to transforming Prague, a formerly provincial town, into an elegant city, not only in appearance, but also by the actions of its each and every citizen. The magazine's ambitions reached beyond the borders of Czechoslovakia, as can be attested by articles published in French since the second year of its existence, and also by the fact that it was distributed by the Hachett company in Paris. Its exe-

Měsíc, cover with a photograph by František Vobecký, Brno 1938

was published on November 15th, 1928. The magazine became a mouthpiece for the ambitions, hopes and fears of the young generation of Czech women. It covered a number of different topics and problems, clothing being one of the most prominent. Its fashion editor Staša Jílovská gave space to young fashion designers who, in constant contact with Parisian fashion and working at the Podolská and Rosenbaum

fashion houses, created a Czech version of European fashion. Over the course of time, Hedvika Vlková, Zdeňka Fuchsová-Mayerová, and Vojtěch Michal published their designs in *Eva*. They managed to maintain the high quality of the tradition of Czech tailoring through the war years into the socialist era, and used their experience in their teaching careers. The magazine also published, especially before the Second World War, designs by other personalities such as E. Süssermannová, M. Kuklová, and M. Langová. Staša Jílovská herself was a supporter of practical, purposeful fashion with a democratic and socially understood approach. Despite this, throughout its existence the magazine had its own contributor in Paris who regularly informed on new developments in Parisian haute couture. The value of the *Eva* magazine was further enhanced by its graphic design which was, in its first two years, the work of František Tichý. Although he was then replaced by Vojtěch Michal and Otakar Fuchs, many other famous artists contributed to the graphic design, such as Antonín Pelc, František Janoušek, Bedřich Piskač, Toyen, and others.

Fashion sections were regularly published in weeklies such as *Český svět* and *Pestrý týden*, as in all big dailies, where they appeared as parts of Saturday and Sunday women's supplements. Besides fashion, they also featured other themes, such as cooking, furnishing, sports, babycare, etc. The contributors were mostly mem-

Gentleman, cover by V. Hrský, December 1926

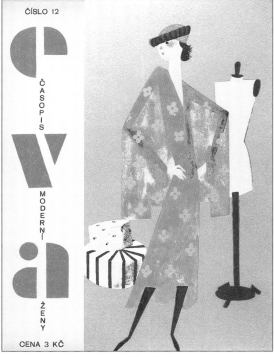

Eva, cover by František Tichý, April 15th, 1934

bers of the young intellectual generation of women who enjoyed a modern lifestyle. A fashion
section in *Lidové noviny* was edited by the energetic and witty Marie Fantová, a daughter of the
famous architect Josef Fanta, who published her
articles under the pseudonym Ma-Fa. Her
articles also appeared in *Elegantní Praha*
in 1924. In *Modní revue*, fashion supplement
of the *Tribuna* newspaper, there was a fashion
section that was edited by Zdenka Watter-son-
Foustková. After
her departure to
the USA, her posi-
tion was assumed
by Milena Jesenská.
At the beginning
of the 1920s, Je-
senská sent her
fashion reports
from Vienna,
which were care-
fully read by Franz
Kafka. Jesenská
soon moved from
Tribuna to a positi-
on as a contribu-
tor to the fashion
and social section
of *Národní listy*.
There she sur-
rounded herself
with a group of
modern young fas-
hion journalists, such as the textile designer
Slávka Vondráčková; a gymnast and propagator of
modern physical education for women and children, Běla Friedländrová; the dancer Milča
Mayerová; Mirina Suchardová; and Zdenka
Wattersonová, who contributed with her articles
from the USA. In 1932, Milena Jesenská accepted
a position on the editing staff of the weekly *Pestrý
týden*, where she joined her long-time friend and
colleague from the Minerva secondary school,
Staša Jílovská, who at the same time worked as
a fashion reporter for *Eva* and *Vkus*. Once again,
Jesenská surrounded herself with experienced
young collaborators, whom she brought from
Národní listy. Besides *Národní listy* and *Pestrý
týden*, Jesenská also worked for *Lidové noviny* and,
from 1931, also for the *Žijeme* magazine,

Portrait of Milena Jesenská

although here not as
a fashion and
women's section
reporter.[77] Her articles
were also scattered
among other magazines
and publications, such as
Gentleman[78] or *Civilisovaná žena*. Her urging voice
was also heard in *Eva*
in the period when the
country faced the threat
of fascism. Jesenská pub-
lished her journalistic articles in two collections
— *Cesta k jednoduchosti (Path to Simplicity)* in 1926
and *Člověk dělá šaty (A Person Makes Clothes)* in
1927. Jesenská did not always concern herself
with fashion alone. Even in her articles specifically
addressed to clothing, fashion was in fact a secondary issue: she was more interested in the lifestyle of the new generation, and considered dress
to be only its expression. This is why Milena Jesenská, in all respects a modern woman, spoke
out with fervour against clothing that was purpo-
seless, complicated, and flashy. "Flashiness is dis-
gusting in any place and at any time, but there,
…where it obstructs, disrupts and only makes
beautiful, it is simply proof of a lower spiritual
level", she wrote. Her thesis, elegantly and clearly

Eva, cover by František Tichý,
July 1st, 1930

Modní revue, cover, August 6th, 1928

Modní revue, cover, April 2nd, 1927

put on paper, expressed the attitude of the interwar generation of middle-class Czech women toward fashion: "Durable and unflashy clothing — the English costume and overcoat, good clothing — will never become boring and poor, it can be restored next year, and something new can be purchased to complement it..." or "The duty to be beautiful is one of the warmest human duties...the difference is to be well dressed or luxuriously dressed...to have more garments than you need is barbaric; it is also barbaric to have several of those garments be ugly". "Beauty can be found in simplicity... There has never been more purposeful and beautiful fashion in the world as today... the sheer simplicity without any adornments and complications. It is progress in every sense of the word, both aesthetic and hygienic."[79]

Fashion journalism was by no means restricted to Prague. Numerous magazines of various kinds, both Czech and German, were published in Brno, a city with a long-standing tradition of textile and clothing production. The towns of Liberec, Podmokly, České Budějovice, Český Těšín, Moravská Ostrava, Litoměřice and others also had their own fashion magazine or fashion supplement.[80]

There were also numerous magazines that were published only for a short time or appeared only to immediately disappear. In fact, the future development of clothing in Bohemia proves that Czech fashion journalism of the 1920s and 1930s substantially influenced the relationship of Czech women toward fashion for many years, at least for two generations.

E. U.

For theatre and dancing balls, Moda a vkus, 1919, no. 6

CHANGES in Fashion 1918· 1924

Fashion in the post-World War I period fluently followed the tendencies of the previous years. Despite the sufferings of war which faced women with a number of new demanding tasks, the development of fashion did not stop during the war-years. Fashion responded to practical necessity with the shortening of skirts to the middle of the calf, and adopted several decorative elements from military uniforms, such as epaulets, buttons, etc. Czech fashion was influenced by the folkloristic movement, (called svéráz) which made its first public appearance at an exhibition in the Community House (Obecní dům) and on Wenceslaus square, no. 50 in the spring of 1915. The aim of this movement was to create a specifically Czech dress drawing inspiration from a rich tradition of Czech folk costumes. Though the distinctive movement declared its independence from international currents of fashion, its character, based on simple and purposeful cuts of national dress, placed it among the most advanced currents in reformist fashion. This is attested by designs of Anna Boudová — Suchardová, Anna Suchardová — Brichová, Anna Dostálová, Marie Lukešová, and Růžena Tillnerová that were published in contemporary women's magazines.[81] Interest in distinction soon shifted from women's to children's fashion. Already in 1919 the first post-war Czechoslovak magazine *Moda a vkus* (*Fashion and Style*) considered distinction as outdated and declared its allegiance to world fashion as a part of a unified world culture.[82]

After the creation of the independent Czechoslovak state in 1918, the political euphoria was expressed not only by the "svéráz" movement, but also by the fact that people commonly wore real folk costumes. Demand for complete or at least partial folk costumes spread every-

SPOLEČENSKÉ ÚBORY

Toiletty večerní vyznačují se nyní hlubokými výstřihy na prsou a zvláště na zádech a sukněmi ozdobnými, bohatě sřasenými anebo dvojitými, jichž dolní objem jest opět velmi úzký. Vrchní sukně (tunika) je širší, splývá v záhybech a vybíhá někdy v cípy. Rukávky jsou krátké, volné, průhledné anebo jich vůbec není.

(Střihy dle míry zašle administrace. Návod k braní míry a kupon k objednávce střihů na zvláštní příloze v tomto sešitě.)

I. Úbor k tanci a do divadla
ze vzorkovaného nebo batikovaného čínského krepu (Crêpe de Chine) s rukávky tylovými nebo muselinovými a pasem z jednobarevného liberty.

II. Společenský a divadelní úbor
z poloprůhledné hedvábné látky, na dolním okraji ručně vyšitý. Sukně a pas z tmavého liberty.

III. Večerní toiletta
ze vzdušné hedvábné látky anebo čínského krepu (Crêpe de Chine), ozdobená tmavými stuhami a perličkovými třásněmi.

Kreslila Tyda Malcová.

Tyda Malcová, Social outfits, Moda a vkus, April 1919

where, especially in big towns where such dress had not been seen for more than a century. The costumes were often combined without regard to their place of origin and compatibility. Folk costumes soon quickly disappeared from everyday life, but for many years were still worn on festive occasions by members of the middle classes everywhere where it was necessary to demonstrate their patriotism, such as during visits of state officials, at Sokol rallies, in the days after World War II, and even as late as the 1950s in communist May Day parades.

Currents in fashion of the first post-war years further developed the style of 1917 with a straight cut complemented by a loose-fitting

Afternoon dress, black silk embroidered with beads, Hana Podolská , around 1919, M. D. A., inv.no. 72.564

ELEGANTNÍ ÚBORY
DENNÍ
K NÁVŠTĚVÁM,
POD PLÁŠŤ

I. Návštěvní a odpolední oblek pod plášť z vlněné látky barvy čekankově modré, ozdobený bílými portami a šňůrkovou výšivkou. Pohled ze předu jest na str. 21. Bluza má volný kimonový střih, vysoký přisazený límec stuartský a zapíná se napřed stiskacími knoflíky na podložený proužek tak, že oba kraje přednic se dotýkají. Sukně je ušitá zvlášť. Základní její tvar je úplně hladký, jen po stranách je našit proužek šikmo střižené látky tak v podobě obráceného ∩, takže se tím sukně na bocích rozšíří. Pas je z téže látky. Rukávy mají dole úzké manžety. — II. Odpolední oblek pod plášť z hnědého hedvábí a sametu ozdobený výšivkou. Sukně je hedvábná, napřed i vzadu jemně strojem skládaná, na bocích tvoří kornoutovité kapsy a jest vyšívaná jak zřejmo z obrázku. Živůtek je z hně=

dého sametu a dosahuje vzadu asi 20 cm. pod pas. Stuartský límec je zvenčí sametový, uvnitř potažený bílým hedvábím. Na ramenou jsou položeny vyšívané hedvábné díly. — III. Odpolední úbor pod plášť ze šedé nebo béžově hnědé vlněné látky, ozdobeným hedvábným pasem téže barvy a velikými knoflíky hedvábím potaženými. Zajímavý je veliký límec, který se může také přeložiti. — IV. Návštěvní šaty pod plášť z vlněné látky tmavomodré nebo tmavozelené, velmi jednoduchého a vkusného tvaru. Výšivka je provedena lesklým silným hedvábím anebo sutaškou. Přeska perleťová. — V. Šaty z vlněné látky se světlou hedvábnou výšivkou. Bluzka v pase volná je napřed krátká, ale po stranách vybíhá až dolů tvoříc sukni, která je napřed otevřena. ⟨Pohledy ze zadu na str. 21.⟩

belt at the waist. At the same time, they took up pre-war styles with barrel-shaped silhouettes. The latter became modern in the next years 1918 — 1919. The barrel-shape was achieved by enlarging the skirt at the hips and tapering it toward the bottom, or by using an additional narrow underskirt. Evening dress, made of tafetta, velvet, and brocade combined with light silk materials (such as tulle, chiffon, lace) had pleated arranged bodices with narrow shoulder straps, or square or v-shaped necks, created by crossing the front parts, which were tied together at the back. Sleeves were usually short and kimono- or bell-shaped. The hems were often decorated with fringes or a row of beads or pearls. The belt was made of a pleated band of fabric, and raised the waistline above its natural level. At the hips, the skirts were fitted with deep, bowl-shaped folds, or gathered or bell-shaped flounces. Also popular were skirts with

a tunic made of a light, airy material, gathered and lengthened at the sides, or, on the contrary, shortened at the sides, with points or flounces. The skirt went down to the middle of the calf. Parisian designs published in the Czech magazine *Moda a vkus* introduced a serpentine-shaped skirt that was twisted around the body of the wearer, a flounce skirt, and a skirt composed of folded wide ribbons pleated over each other vertically like flower petals to form a barrel-shape. Special two-coloured ribbons were supposedly made in Paris especially for this purpose. An oddity was a skirt with a circle at the waist, which resembled Spanish Renaissance skirts. Historical inspiration can be detected in a number of models: wide necklines extending past the shoulders and gathered overskirts both recalled the Biedermeier style. Stand-up collars, used in all kinds of dresses, from evening dresses to suits and coats, were marked as of the Stuart style. Dresses flowing from the left shoulder to the right hip, complemented by drapery, resembled Roman togas. High waistlines and double-breasted buttoning evoked the Directoire style. Kimono cuts of dresses, coats, and raincoats, and certain kinds of ornamentation reveal a Japanese inspiration.

Afternoon wear was simpler, sewn of silk or woolen fabrics. They often combined single-colour materials with checkered, striped or other-patterned materials. The bodice had falling shoulders, was semi-fitted, somewhat bunched, with a high turned or Stuart standing collar and with sleeves that were either of a kimono cut or set into extended opening. The fashionable widening of the sides on heavy coat dresses was achieved by setting in funnel-shaped side pieces in which there were pockets. Light woolen materials produced bowl-shaped folds at the hips. In the years 1920 — 21, the barrel shape lost its fulness and the straight, loose-fitting line grew more widespread. Shirt dresses became fashionable; they were divided or partially divided at waist level, fitted with a very loose belt slightly above the waistline. In fashion magazines they were denoted as "smock" dresses. They were used as both formal and informal wear, as is shown in a photograph of Růžena Nasková in

H. Piskáčková-Hanušová, subretta Měst. divadla vinohradského, v černém malém kloboučku ozdobeném černými křídly.
Z dílen M. Kreisingrové.

Odpolední úbory šijí se i letos s oblibou v celku a mají často rovný, nepřiléhavý tvar. Charakteristická pro letošní plášťový oblek jest dvojí sukně, vrchní kratší, spodní užší a delší. Výstřih u krku ponechává se letos volný, bez límce. Pás ovinuje postavu zcela volně a jest zavázán vzadu ve vázanku.

Foto Vácha.

Foto Vácha.

Slaměný klobouček zdobený tmavými křídly.
Z dílen M. Kreisingrové.

Nejenom veliké, ale i zcela malé kloboučky se letos nosí. Přiléhají pevně na malý účes a nasazují se hluboko do očí — dle vkusu buďto rovně anebo šikmo. Zdobí se křídly neb stuhami nebo se pokrývají jejich dýnka květinami. Malý klobouček jest určen pouze k denním vycházkám, pro večer hodí se lépe klobouky široké.

Růžena Nasková, člen Nár. divadla, v pastelově modrém úboru, ozdobeném hedvábnou stříbrošedou výšivkou a zhotoveném v dílnách H. Podolské.

Růžena Nasková in afternoon dress from the Hana Podolská fashion house, Moda a vkus, April 1919, photograph by Vácha

Gaston:

HIGH LIFE.

Král Eduard VII. byl, jak známo, nejenom králem Velké Britanie, nýbrž i králem mody. První úloha byla jistě velice snadná, neboť býti králem Anglickým není zaměstnáním tak těžkým a zodpovědným jako býti presidentem republiky, ať na příkl. francouzské nebo třeba naší. Anglický král je v první řadě hlavou společnosti, nejurozenějším lordem říše a osobností representativní. Býti králem mody jest úloha obtížnější, jež skončila u jiných než korunovaných hlav, jež nevládly nesčetnými a nevyčerpatelnými zdroji finančními, skoro vždy tragicky a nejméně duševním i materielním bankrotem. Vzpomeňme slavného a duchaplného Brummela, jenž zemřel opuštěn a v bídě, nezapomeňme na hořký úděl Oscara Wildea. — Balzac marně se snažil po celý život jíti podobnou cestou.

O Eduardovi lze ovšem říci vše spíše než že by byl vržen jen sebemenší stín tragičnosti na jeho životní dráhu. Kdo jej ještě pamatuje, jak si vykračoval, bonhomní a korektní po promenádě v Mariánských lázních, jistě mi dá za pravdu. A při tom se oblékal tak pečlivě a vymyšleně, že na to nikdo jiný ... Začal jsem o něm proto, abych Vám ... z jeho tajemství, jež značně přispělo ... jal v paměti všech, kdož mají pocho-

peni pro to, co je pravý high life, místo na něm dosud trůní. Dozvěděl jsem se toto tajemství skrétnosti jednoho podřadného ind ... francouzského.

Eduard nikdy neoblékl nových šatů. Jeho krejčí zaměstnával zvláště vyhledaného muže, jehož postav byla přesně stejná jako postava králova. Každý oblek tvrdosti a apretury a pak jej teprve oblékl král ... musil tento muž nejdříve obnositi z jeho počáteč ... Znáte ze zkušenosti, jak se nový oblek skládá v tvrdé záhyby, jak se láme a muchlá a jak starý oblek mile přilehne a skládá se v elegantní, dobré záhyby.

Je v tom jedno z nejdůležitějších pravidel pravé elegance. Vyžehlenost a nonchalance se nesnášely.

Na muži, jenž chce býti opravdu elegantním, nesmí nikdy býti viděti, že nosí nové šaty.

Indiskretní lokálkář mluví též o kloboucích a prozrazuje, že dvojník králův musil klobouk vždy nositi celou sezónu, než jej král vzal na hlavu. To však prý platilo jen pro měkké klobouky. Nevím, zda je byl osobní vliv Eduardův, jenž pak vytvořil tradici, že dobrý klobouk nesmí býti nový. V Praze se tento princip v poslední době nepochopil a kloboučníci i mladí elegáni musejí komplikovaně své klobouky, na nichž je viděti, že jsou nové. To je ovšem omyl.

Letos se tyto vzpomínky na krále mody stávají více aktuelnimi, neboť

Ada Roubíčková: Návrhy toilet mody 1923-24.

Ada Roubíčková , Designs for toilettes — fashion of 1923/24, Elegantní Praha,

Dámské Modní Listy, 1920

Afternoon dress from the Hana Podolská fashion house,
Elegantní Praha, October 1922

a dress from the salon of Hana Podolská from the year 1919.[83] This straight loose-fitting cut further developed with layering of separate pieces of clothing, their combination and over-laying. Dresses not only had a double skirt, but a long or short pinafore could be worn over the whole dress at the front and back. A loose-fitting shirt-front could be worn over the bodice. In addition, a bolero or vest could be suggested. Smock dresses could be cut in the shape of a long open cossack dress or could have an opening in the front in which there was a central pleated section. The effect of this architectonic cut was enhanced by the combination of single coloured and patterned fabrics. Embroidery was increasingly incorporated into the designs.

In the course of 1921, skirts started to become longer and the waistline shifted to the hips. Informal wear from Prague fashion workshops which was modelled by actresses and ladies from Prague high society was loose-fitting with turned up bodice, slightly lowered waistline, and frilled skirt complemented by a tunic, points, and draperies. Despite a modern cut and a number of interesting details, such as richly tailored sleeves, this elegant Parisian fashion did not lend itself to the Slavic figures of Czech ladies. Over time, informal wear became simpler and narrower, its width now determined by the hips of the wearer, and it was often undivided at the waistline. And what underwear did Czech women wear in this period? Loose-fitting clothing did not demand the deformation of the wearer's body by corsets. *Moda a vkus* magazine in 1919 reported that Parisian women wore only elastic bands instead of corsets because the figure of a lady no longer had to resemble a puppet. As the import of these elastic bands to Czechoslovakia was forbidden, bands were made in the style of narrow bodices with buttoning at the front.[84] The bands were complemented by uncom-

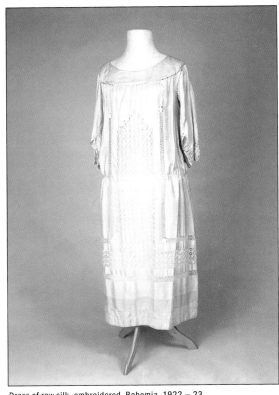

Dress of raw silk, embroidered, Bohemia, 1922 – 23, M. D. A. , inv. no. 91.106

Elegantní Praha, 1924

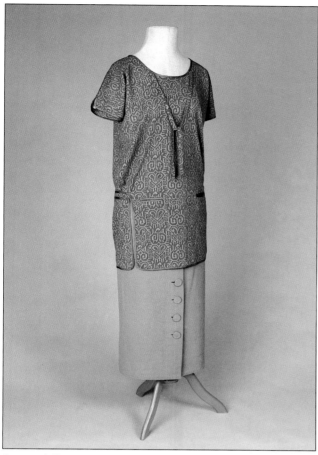

Costume of skirt and cossack jacket, Bohemia around 1924, M. D. A.,
inv.no. 51.593 and 51.594

kind of clothing. In later years they took the
form of buttoned vests used instead of jackets,
or the form of jumpers — longish pullovers with
a small neckline usually with a belt and pockets.
Sweaters, of course, were also a part of sports-
wear, especially of ski outfits. In the early 1920s,
ski outfits were composed of narrow trousers,
enlarged at the hips, a sweater, and a coat with
a high collar and many pockets, complemented
by a knitted wrapper and cap. Among the designs of Anna Lukášová from 1919 was a ski outfit consisting of a short pleated skirt and admi-
rable modern and practical "coat for a
snowstorm". The coat was made of waterproof
material and had a raglan cut with a hood and
belt that passed underneath sewn on pockets.
Suits, though expensive, were very widespread.
In 1919 — 20, a suit-jacket called "cutaway",
was extended to three-quarter length; the hips
were emphasized by folds or gathering at the
waist. Protruding coat-tails recalled the coats
of Baroque men's outfits. The front pieces were
tightly closed, with double-breasted buttoning
or single-breasted side buttoning as well as
shawl, Stuart, or high stand-up collars. The suits
were strikingly decorated with furs — wide borders, whole panels or sets of high cuffs and collars. In later years the emphasis of the hips disappeared. Women now wore suits with classical
cuts or dinner jackets with elongated lapels and

plicated bras and trouser or skirt slips with bell-
shaped panties. A new kind of women's underwear designed for sleeping in and as morning
wear was the pyjama.

The rapid growth in women's emancipation and
ever growing influence of sport encouraged the
turn to a practical sytle in daily wear. Well-sui-
ted for the workplace was a shirt dress, as was
a skirt with blouse, complemented by a sweater,
or a cossack dress, composed of a straight skirt
and a cossack — a long uncut blouse with small
neckline or collar.

Very fashionable was a three-piece suit — "robe
de trois pièces" — composed of a skirt, blouse,
usually of cossack shape, and a jacket. Also fashionable was a two-piece suit consisting of
a dress and jacket. Jersey fabrics and handmade
knitwear became popular. Sweaters appeared in
Moda a vkus magazine in 1919 as a rather new

"Pyjama, a new type of women's sleeping and morning dress", drawing by Anna Lukášová, Moda a vkus, 1919, no. 6

Pohledy ze zadu ke všem úborům jsou na str. 22.

closed with a single button at the waist. Around 1923 the waistline became looser and styles appeared that corresponded to the straight line of the 1920s, such as single or double-buttoned trotteur with straight cut elongated cutaway. There also appeared a blouse jacket buttoned and gathered at one side.

The shape of overcoats also corresponded to contemporary styles of fashion. In 1919 they consisted of a kimono-cut closed with a single button, or a cape cut with undifferentiated sleeves. The barrel-shape silhouette was created by lowered shoulders and enlarged hips. After 1920, overcoats became increasingly straight, closed at the neck, with a high folded collar. The overcoat was loose-fitting, with single or double-breasted buttoning, and with or without a belt.

Fur coats were popular throughout the 1920s. Since they varied in price depending on the kind of fur used, they were accessible to girls and women of all classes. The cost of purchasing such coats was not significantly greater than of a winter coat. Short fur coats were worn for sports, travel, car-rides, and walks, since they accorded to the fashionable sporty style.

Costume of dress and jacket, violet marocain, Maison Eckstein, Prague 1922 – 23, M. D. A., inv.no. 93.252

Luxurious fur coats were made of Persians with skunk fur, of breitschwantz with chinchilla, seal with opposum or mink, whose furs were decoratively combined into geometric patterns.

The type of dress in which contemporary ideas of fashion are always most evident are small and full evening wear. This was particularly evident in the first half of the 1920s, a period which, in historical terms, was given the name "Art Deco" for its decorative aesthetic principles.

There were two silhouettes of evening wear: the first was a long, narrow sheath dress with a lowered and only slightly emphasized waistline; the second, the so-called style dress, had a tight-fitting bodice with a waist lower than the natural waistline and wide crinoline skirt with flounces and pleats. The cut of the first, straight silhouette dress in fact consisted of two long bands of fabric shaped in various manners at the hips and skirt. The fabric could be gathered at the left hip, thus raising and shortening the point of the skirt, or, on the contrary, a longer piece could be set into pleats, creating the point of a train.

Costume of skirt and cossack jackets, Bohemia around 1924, M. D. A., inv.no. 51.595 and 51.594

omilá a vždy s vybraným vkusem se odívající slečna Machová, člen Měst. divadla vinohradského, dala se fotografovat ve svých sweatrech, které ji tak dobře sluší. Její obrázky jsou důkazem, jak elegantní je tato rně nová součástka dámské garderoby, která nad jiné dobře doplní lehké úbory za chladných jarních večerů. ábné sweatry bývají doplněny šálou, která se ovinuje kolem krku. Sweatr jest elegantní náhražkou za plaid aneb vlněný šátek.

Foto Schumpeter.

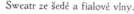

bný sweatr bílý s černými pruhy.

Sweatr ze šedé a fialové vlny.

"Knitted silk and woolen jackets (sweaters)",
Moda a vkus, April 1919, photograph by Schumpeter

Anna Lukášová, Designs of sporting garments,
Moda a vkus, 1919, no. 6

ZIMNÍ SPORT

III. ⟨Nahoře.⟩ Lyžecký oblek pro mladé dívky. Vlněný sweatr, čepice a šála jsou ozdobené bílými vlněnými třásněmi. Vzor na šále a swea‑ tru jest šedý a šmolkově modrý. Sukně šedě pruhovaná jest skládaná tak, že šedé pruhy jsou skryté v záhybech. Bílé vlněné rukavice. — IV. ⟨Nahoře.⟩ Lyžecký dres po norském způ‑ sobu, zhotovený z nepromokavého tmavomo‑ drého sukna. Kabát je ušit na způsob vojenské bluzy, ale bez pasu , může se však doplniti pa‑ sem z téhož sukna anebo koženým. Spodky jsou ušité v celku s kamašemi a zapínají se na obou bocích. — V. ⟨Dole.⟩ Sportovní vesta z duvetynu barvy terakotové, lemovaná bílou kůží. Kalhoty sportovní z kostkované teplé lát‑ ky. — V. Sportovní kabátek do sněhové vánice z nepromokavého plátna s praktickými kapsami a kapucí. Vlněná čapka barvy béžové a fialové.

Pohledy ze zadu ke všem úborům jsou na stránce 22.

Šebestian Kellner, Designs for girls' dresses for walking,
Pražská moda, spring—summer 1924

D 10.
Návrhy Š. Kellnera.

1. **D í v č í   v y c h á z k o v ý   ú b o r** sestává
ze sukně vlněné s rypsovými pruhy. Kabátek
jest z lehké látky jednobarevné, zdobený vý-
šivkovými pruhy. Může však býti z červené, bílé a modré vlny. K tomuto kostýmku
může býti zhotoven i šálový pruh, zdobený
výšivkou. Velmi apartní klobouček z hnědého
pedalu, jehož největší zvláštností jest jeho
zcela nový tvar, zdoben jest ze strany růžicí
z hnědých a mořsky modrých rypsových stu-
žek. Skupinka jich splývá roztomile do vý-
seku kloboučku a lehounce se dotýká kadeří.
Model ten jest od fy. G. M ü l l e r , P r a h a ,
O p a t o v i c k á 26. Tato firma chystá pro léto
a zvláště pro lázně tak krásné a originelní kloboučky, že bude jistě jako roku minulého hlavní
představitelkou „Pražské Mody". A tak jako
loni zaplavila jimi přímo všechny lázně, hlavně
přímořské, tak také letos těmito chystanými novin-
kami vzbouří všechny dámské kruhy, jichž heslem
je elegance.

2. **S u k n ě   a   j u p i č k a.** Sukně může býti
tmavěžlutá se zelenými proužky neb šedá s černými proužky. Jupička, jež má velmi apartní
stojatý límeček, může býti z červeného lamé se
zlatem. K tomu velmi krásný klobouček z tmavo-
hnědého hedvábí, jehož stříška jest barevná.
Model ten jest od fy. G. M ü l l e r , P r a h a ,
O p a t o v i c k á 26.

3. **O d p o l e d n í   š a t y** ze šedého crep ty-
rolien neb z crep georgetu. Úplně nový útvar
kapsy jakož i pásek, který volně splývá od
kapsy, jest ze zeleného hedvábí. Klobouček
z jemné rýžové slámy, jevící velmi originelní
střední ozdobu hlavičky, jest od fy. G. M ü l l e r,
P r a h a, O p a t o v i c k á 26.

K ZIMNÍM VYCHÁZKÁM

I. Kostym z vlněného veluru barvy světle hnědé nebo šedé, lemovaný vydří kožišinou. Střih tohoto žaketu je zcela nový, šos je na bocích skládaný. Ke kostýmu náleží rukávník z téže kožišiny, jako lem žaketu. Vysoký límec, zapíná se na levé straně a jest rovněž olemován kožišinou. Žaket zapíná se na poutka ze šňůrek a knoflíky potažené látkou, po případě také na knoflíky rohové v barvě kožišiny. — II. Plášť z vlněného veluru barvy zelené, ozdobený kožišinovým límcem šálovým.

Tento plášť má velmi oblíbený volný tvar plášťřenkový (cape, khép). Sestaven je ze dvou částí: horní, ze které vybíhá vrchní díl rukávů, a dolní, která tvoří napřed ostré špičky, vsazené až k ramenům. Plášť jest podšit hedvábnou podšívkou vzorkovanou. — IV. Kostym z jemné gabardiny barvy temně modré, velmi jednoduchý a vkusný, ozdobený lesklými černými hedvábnými portami. Rovný žaket má šálový dlouhý límec liščí. Manžety a rukávník z téže kožišiny.

Pohledy ze zadu jsou na str. 20.

"For winter walks", Moda a vkus, 1919, no. 6

Dámské Modní Listy, 1920

The outer garment could form a shortened tunic twisting around the body or creating points that onetheless did not disturb the straight silhouette of the garment. The train sometimes flowed from the shoulders as loose drapery. The dresses were usually undivided, fitted with an oval boat neck or v-neck created by crossing the front parts of the garment. Dresses often had only narrow shoulder straps. Front and back parts did not have to be sewn together — they could form a sheath connected only at the hips and worn over another garment. The dresses were usually sleeveless; if they did have sleeves, it was only for decoration. The sleeves could be short, deeply cut and joined at the shoulders and wrists, the loose parts forming more drapery. Between 1921 — 1924 evening wear reached to the ankles.

The decorative and luxurious character of fabric was perhaps the product of a reaction to the hardship and suffering of the war years. In addition to classic materials used for evening wear, such as tulle, tafeta, velour-chiffon, and chiffon, it was popular to use fabrics that were interwoven with metal fibres, brocades, moirã interwoven with metal, and gold-printed fabrics. Textured fabrics with impressed and interwoven patterns, such as matlasé or velour-chiffon broché, formed a velvet-like pattern on a smooth chiffon background. The decorative effect of these splendid fabrics and patterns was further enhanced by embroidery that was usually executed with beads or little pearls. Embroidery was used in borders, in both individual motifs and whole fields. The huge demand for embroidery of this kind stimulated the creation of a new decorative technique in which beads or paste stones were stamped directly into the fabric. Another kind of decoration involved applications of silk and velvet,

Tdl. D. III.

L. Melková-Ondrušová , Designs for skirts and costumes with
blouses, Pražská moda, spring—summer 1924

Afternoon overcoat of brown velour-chiffon, embroidered,
the Rosenbaum fashion house, Elegantní Praha, November—
December 1923, photograph by Schlosser and Wenisch, Prague

Evening toilettes from the Podolská fashion house, Elegantní Praha, December 1922, photograph by F.Drtikol and Co.

Overcoat of linen or velour, embroidered, collar and cuffs of breitschwantz, Pražská moda, autumn—winter 1923/24

fantastic and imaginary artificial flowers, as well as ostrich and marabou feathers. The decorative tendencies were also used on hidden parts of garments, such as in the lining of evening coats, which were interwoven with gold and silver fibres.

Furs were another important decorative element. They were used on all kinds of dresses, both formal and walking wear. Long-haired furs, such as fox and monkey, were used for formal evening wear, while short-haired furs covered collars, cuffs, and sometimes entire pieces of suits and overcoats to produce an ornamental effect.

Embroidery was not limited to evening wear. It was also used on informal wear, suits, and overcoats, always corresponding to the type of garment. Inspiration for the ornamentation was diverse: geometric or folk ornamentation of the Balkan nations was used on informal wear, while oriental or historicizing patterns were used for formal evening wear. Egyptian-style ornamentation even appeared in the Czech lands, made popular by the discovery of the tomb of Tutankhamen in 1922.

Evening toilette of yellow silk and gold lace, embroidered with beads, Prague around 1923, M. D. A., inv.no. 91.492

Afternoon dress, black wool with violet embroidery, Prague around 1923
M. D. A., inv.no. 84.800

Summer dress of white batiste, white embroidery, colourfully embroidered belt,
the Zádruha association, 1921 – 24, M. D. A., inv.no. 47.935

Evening overcoat from the Hana Podolská fashion house. Elegantní Praha, November 1924,
photograph by F. Drtikol and Co.

In this period of searching for new sources of decorative style of clothing, when the interest of world designers shifted to the folk art especially of the Balkan countries, distinctive elements once again appeared in the Czech lands. The production of the Zádruha association also belongs to this style of decorativism. From its establishment in 1900, Zádruha produced embroidered garments with simple and fashionable cuts which were decorated with white and coloured embroidery of folk character. A dress from the workshop of Hana Podolská is of particular interest: it had scroll ornamentation recalling motifs of Czech bonnet ribbons. Paul Poiret, during his visit to Prague in 1923, considered this ornament to be the hit of the next fashion season in Paris.[85]

Foto Drtikol a spol.

Persianový plášť se skunkem
ZE SALONU KOŽIŠIN JOSEF BÁRTA, VINOHRADY,
Havlíčkova třida číslo 4,
(Mikovcova 9).

Persian overcoat with skunk from the Josef Bárta fur salon, Vinohrady.
Elegantní Praha, November 1924. Photography by F. Drtikol and Co.

ELEGANTNÍ PRÁDLO.

Barevné prádlo

z batistu, čínského krepu neb praciho hedvábí zdobí se krajkou silně žlutého tónu, neb aplikací odlišné barvy.

W 1165. Košil. spodky s odlišnou aplikací. Stř. vel. I., II. a III. dodá admin. za 6 Kč.

W 1087. Košil. spodky zdobené krajkou a pecičkami. Stř. vel. I., II. a III. dodá admin. za 6 Kč.

W 1082. Živůtková spodnička se záhyby. Stř. vel. I., II., III. a IV. dodá admin. za 6 Kč.

W 1208. Souprava: denni košile a spodky. Stř. vel. I., II. a III. dodá adm. za 6 Kč.

W 1188. Košil. spodky zvonov. tvaru. Stř. vel. I., II. a III. dodá admin. za 6 Kč.

W 1201. Elegantní noční košile bez rukávů. Stř. vel. I., II. a III. dodá adm. za 6 Kč.

W 1201   W 1188

W 1087. Košil. spodky. Jasně zelený opál. batist tvoří materiál k těmto košilovým spodkům, opatřeným v pasové čáře stahovadlem, jež se protáhne stuhou. K okrajům se průsvitně přisadí krajk. vložka, krajka ohraničuje všecky okraje. Mezi tím a na ramenou nalézá se pecičková výšivka. V rozkroku závěrka knofliky. Spotř. (vel. II.): 160 cm látky, 100 cm šir.

W 1208. Souprava prádla ze šeříkově fial. batistu a žlutavé krajky má originelní střih spodků, nahoře opatřených stahovadlem, dole k vyzubov. okraji krajka a po stranách vázanka ze stuhy. Spotř.: 265 cm látky, 80 cm šir.

W 1201. Elegantní noční košile bez rukávů. Barevný krep čínský a žlutá krajka dvou různých šířek sloužily ku zhotovení elegantní noční košile, jejíž dolní lemovka jest přisazena ažurou. Stuha do pasu..

W 1188. Košil. spodky. Úplně novy tvar přináší naše vyobraz., na němž jest dolní část košil. spodků střižena do zvonu a přisazena zubatě k horni hladké části. K ozdobě krajka. V rozkroku závěrka knofliky. Spotř.: 150 cm hedvábí, 100 cm šir.

W 1165. Košil. spodky z lila batistu jsou zakončeny nahoře i dole lemovkou z bílého tylu. Dole závěrka dírkovou patkou a záklopkou. Výšivka je aplikována bílým batistem a provedena bílou lesklou přízí. Spotř. (vel. II.): 150 cm látky, 80 cm šir.

W 1082. Živůtková spodnička z růžového hedváb. krepu nemá ozdob, jen ručně provedenou užuru. Po stranách jsou složené záhyby. Spotř. (vel. II.): 230 cm krepu, 100 cm šir.

1925-1928

Fashion of the second half of the 1920s was sporty and practical. Individual types of clothes of course were differentiated according to their function. Nevertheless, all kinds of garments save for formal evening wear were influenced by the sporty style. Fashion was determined by practical garments for the work place, trips to the countryside, and sports.

The most popular examples of this style were suits of the most diverse types. In contrast to previous conceptions, where individual parts were related by purpose rather than design, the suits were now made of two or more kinds of fabrics and were covered with the same kind of decoration. In the case of a suit consisting of a two-piece dress and coat, for example, the fabric of the coat was used on the skirt and also decorated the blouse, while the second fabric appeared on the blouse and as decoration on the coat. The suit was decorated with straps, bands, decorative edging, patterned flaps and pockets, etc. Materials of various colours were combined, such as mono-coloured with patterned — especially checkered and striped — fabrics. Around 1927, a new combination of woolen and silk, and alternatively jersey, fabric appeared. The advantage of these new combinations was their great variability as well as their minimal cost, since it was possible to acquire a modern dress made from scraps of material and resewn older garments.

There were a great number of suits. In addition to suits with dresses and overcoats, a kind of suit was still worn in which the dress was made of the same material as the lining of the overcoat. A formal suit appropriate for afternoon visits to a café or concert could consist of overcoat and skirt made from the same material, such as velvet, complemented by an elegant silk blouse that hung over the skirt and was belted. Another suit, considered in 1927 to be ideal for the city, consisted of a bell-shaped skirt, jersey pullover, small vest with pockets and belt, and a raglan overcoat.

Short or three-quarter length jackets and pelerines of various cuts also found application as parts of suits. A definitely sporty kind of suit consisted of a short skirt, often pleated, an English blouse with a man's tie, and a knitted vest with sleeves. Fashion magazines recommended trouser skirts as a variation. The trouser skirt appeared as a new hit at the fashion show of Hana Podolská in 1927, but it does not seem to have become widespread. The knitted vest could be replaced with a vest made of cloth, duvetine, velvet, jersey, or even of silk or leather. Winter vests could be lined with quilting or made of fur.

Suits at this time were so popular that they somewhat pushed to the side classic costumes. The latter adjusted themselves to suits — for example, the coat was made from a different material than the skirt. Costumes also adopted

Black costume decorated with white fabric,. the Matějovský fashion house. Elegantní Praha, April 1925. Photograph by F.Drtikol and Co.

Praktický oblek k cestování.

S 1038. Vycházkový oblek sportovního tvaru. Stř. vel.
a III. dodá admin. za 8 Kč.

S 1037. Vycházkový oblek se sakovou jupičkou. Stř. vel. I., II.
a III. dodá admin. za 8 Kč.

M 981. Pláštěnka k šatům. Stř. vel. I., II. a III. dodá admin.
za 8 Kč.

S 1037. Vycházkový oblek se sakovou jupičkou, zhotovený ze vzorované kostým. látky, která vyhlíží jako proplétaná, ale jest silnější a odolnější nežli tato. Sukně jest rovná a prostá s úzkou pasovkou. Jupička opatřená stran. kapsami a náprsní kapsou má záševek vybíhající s ramen.

M 981. Pláštěnka k šatům K 3129. Jumprové šaty vyobr. v pozadí, jichž sukně jest sežehlená v protilehlé záhyby a přisazená ke kulatému sedlu a jejichž jumper obléká se přes hlavu o sobě, jsou doplněny polodlouhou pláštěnkou v oblek. Táž má dopředu přesahující sedlo a připevní se k šatům spínátky. Spotř. (vel. II.): 260 cm lát. k šatům, 165 cm k pláštěnce, v šířce 130 cm.

S 1038. Vycházkovy oblek sport. tvaru. Tento oblek, opatřený přepásanou jupičkou, k němuž jest třeba vzorov. anglic. látky, má na sukni ze čtyř pol sestávající opět oblíbené sklepní švy, jež se opakují vzadu na jupičce, tvoříce se sukní jednu linii. Kapsy jsou připnuty knoflíkem. Sponami protažený pás.

M 991. Plášť do nečasu. Nové impregnované hedvábí, zvané »dešťové«, sloužilo ke zhotovení tohoto raglán. pláště, který jest velice lehoučký. Možno jej ovšem zhotoviti i z jiných látek, jako burbery nebo gabardiny, hlavní věcí zůstane, že jest látka nepromokavá a plášť možno nositi bez deštníku.

M 992. Pláštěnkový plášť z kostkov. impregnované látky má velice slušivý tvar. Pláštěnka jest vzadu vystřižena až k sedlu a k plášti pevně přisazena. Vpředu má plášť kapsy a zapíná se na jeden knoflík.

Nutno pamatovati také na deštivé dny.

M 991. Plášť do nečasu s beder. rukávy a přesk. pásem
vel. I., II., III. dodá admin. za 8 Kč.

M 992. Pláštěnkový plášť z kostkov. látky na cesty. Stř.
III., IV. dodá adm. za 8 Kč.

Veškeré vzory, střihy a nákresy kvyobrazením dodá na požádání administrace za obnos předem zasl

Strana 26. ELEGANTNÍ PRAHA *Číslo 2.*

Modely z jarní přehlídky paní **HANNY PODOLSKÉ** *v Praze-Lucernč.*
Lázeňské šaty z bílého krepu vyšité černými, žlutými | *Kostým z modrého rypsu s černými prolamovanými*
a oranžovými knoflíčky. Bílý sametový klobouk třírohý | *portami. Černá rýžová toca s gragrain stuhou.*
s pestrou stuhou. | *Foto Drtikol a spol. Praha.*

Elegantní Praha, April 1925, photograph by F. Drtiko and Co.l

**White tenis dress with trouser skirt, Brno, the Hartmann fashion house,
around 1925. M. D. A. inv.no. 91.121**
**"Sporty" jacket of purple- white checked woolen fabric, Prague, the
Roubíčková fashion house, around 1925. M. D. A.,inv.no. 86.431**

"Practical outfit for travelling." Modní svět, July 5th, 1926

the sporty style, the coat reaching to slightly past the hips and with a closed standing or shawl collar at the neck. The skirts were narrow and short just below the knees. The overcoat had a straight cut and was either loose-fitting or girded at the hips. Popular were shawl collars created by long-haired pelt of otter, beaver, or fox.

Other popular types of dress which could be used for different occasions were two-piece jumper suits, combining skirts and a long blouse of different materials. Knitted or knitwear jumpers complemented classic English costumes and suits with trousers, which were designed for hiking, cycling, motorcycle riding, and skiing.

Besides suits of sporty character, which were often worn for less formal evening occasions, classic informal and formal evening suits prevailed. Their cut did not substantially change; they continued to reach slightly below the knees, were loose-fitting, with the waistline lowered to the hips, and had a tucked up bodice. Around the year 1926 the skirt became looser and was flared, with inset folds at the hips, pleats, or bell-shaped pieces. There was an effort to return the waistline to its natural position with the aid of wide bands. A change of the straight and simple style that had til now been prevalent was first detected in 1927 with the introduction of certain irregularities, such as a skirt diagonally set to the bodice, irregular placement of pleats on the skirt, uneven hemlines of the skirt, the asymmetric design of necklines, or the placement of shawls and wraps on only one side of the wearer's body.

Evening wear retained its decorative character provided by luxurious materials, cuts, and rich embroidery. The suits could be straight and narrow, either with an enlarged skirt with inset pieces, or with a wide bell-shaped, gathered or flounced crinoline skirt. In 1927 skirts of varying length were made; they were shorter in the front than in the back, widened with bell-shaped pieces, folds, or pleats. This trend was also confirmed by the fashion show La Haute Couture de Paris, which was organized by the Alliance Française de Prague as part of the Prague Sampling Fair. Renowned Parisian fashion houses like Worth, Lanvin, Philippe et Gaston, Callot, Chernit, Jenny presented collections of evening toilettes primarily of stylish character with

módní linie

halenkovitá plnost nahoře.

M 1046. Plášť z námoř. modr.

M 1039. Plášť nového, po stra-

M 1051. Plášť z marengo se

Na několika pláštích vidím
zdůrazněnou tuto novou mód
Změnou v módě jest také fan
hotovení zadku na nových mo
V předešlých letech byl zadek
dnes jest rozdělení sedlového t
značně sřasené přisazenou dol
na denním pořádku a sedlovi
mění se v pestré řadě mezi r
projmutými nebo různě vybí
tvary. Dnes platí hlavně názor -
pokud možno nejvíce rozstřiham
přímo mistrně sesazovaná. Velk
hu zde hrají obloučky všech tva
ché, vysoké, kulaté i špičaté. Č
šaty elegantnější, tím jest zpr
jejich komplikovanější. Hladký
výstřih vidíme jen ještě na m
vyhlížejících šatech k tanci,
rovný, košil. límec na praktick
poledních šatech. Ale na elegan
šatech, jak je nosíváme odpole
držujeme se spíše špičatého
který se táhne až k pásu. Šálov
platí za novinku, jeho dlouhé k
často svazují, což je móda v
bivá a předpovídá se jí delšíh
Také šálový límec z kožišiny
letos přísně rovné linie límce l
Přes to však nezatlačil úplně te
ný límec, který jsa vztyčen
mnohé ženské hlavě slušivé
V kožišinových druzích, kter
k bohaté výzdobě zimních pláš
cházkových obleků, nastala
změna. Po přibarvování kožiš
stínu látky šatů, při čemž se
nezalekli ani barvy zelené a

Mrs. Marie Venturová,a wife of the olympic champion, in formal social outfit of overcoat and jumper dress, Prague, around 1926. Photograph by Balzar

Outfit – dress of beige georgette and overcoat of beige woolen fabric with fur collar, the Rosenbaum fashion house, 1927, M. D. A., inv.no. 73.230

simple bodices wrapping the bosom, often faste-ned only at one shoulder, and with skirts that at the back reached down to the heels or featured long points of light transluscent fabrics. A new feature that found great admiration was a gold dinner jacket worn over a black stylish toilette.[86] The same excitement was generated by the fas-hion show of the Hana Podolská fashion house that took place several weeks before the French show. Here also appeared ladies' evening dinner jacket, this time made of silver lamé. A fashion journalist did not report on the cuts of the dres-ses, but concentrated on the beauty of the ma-terials on designs with such romantic names as "Venezia" — a black tafetta crinoline embroide-red with motifs of ribbons made of diamonds — or "Aragonese" — a toilette of navy-blue lace-work interwoven with gold. The dresses were complemented by covers, wrappers, and scarves that were richly embroidered with gaily-colou-red blooms and edged with gold, as well as by evening coats and capes of velour-chiffon with high collars inspired by the period of Catherine Medici. The ultimate luxury were furs of all kinds: covers of silver fox, mink stoles and all-fur coats, including ones combining breitschwantz and persian, seal and bisam, pithanic, as well as mink at a price of 75,000 crowns.[87]

The year 1928 saw a change toward a more fe-minine style of clothing. After a period in which woman had expressed their position in society by their dress, women now wanted to demon-strate that their efforts at emancipation had not deprived them of their feminine grace and ten-derness.[88] These tendencies provoked the criti-ism of Czech avantgarde artists, who felt that the purposefulness and democratic character of

Evening dress of green georgette, embroidered with sequins and beads, Prague, the Strnad fashion house, around 1926, M.D. A., inv.no. 88.157

Outfit – dress and jacket of purple poplin and brown-red-purple striped knitwear with asymetrically designed neckline and skirt, Prague, around 1927, M. D. A., inv.no. 87.347

fashion that had been attained in clothing in the 1920s, was in danger of being lost. They blamed commercial reasons of the French fashion industry for such tendencies. In 1929, they called for purposeful and democratic women's dress in the publication *Civilisovaná žena*. They regarded trouser suit as the only form of modern women's dress.

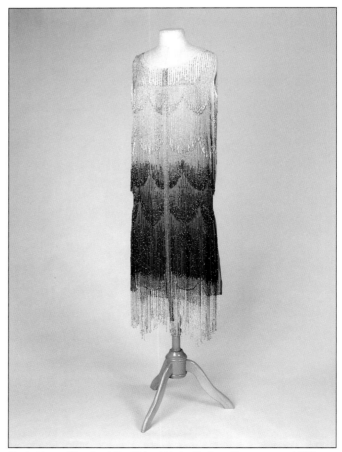

Evening dress of blue georgette with bead fringes, Prague or Olomouc, around 1925, M. D. A., inv.no. 82.381

Modní revue, cover, March 26th, 1927

1929 • 1936

A surprise at the Paris fashion shows of the autumn of 1929 were long skirts. Several designers claimed to have introduced them: Jean Patou made this claim in the December 1930 issue of *Eva* magazine; several weeks later the same claim was made by Jean Philippe Worth, who nevertheless justified the turn to long skirts as an unconscious yearning of women for a return to femininity and elegance. He ascribed the previous fashion of short skirts and short hair to the influence of the war which, after ten years, women finally wanted to forget.[89]

Long skirts were the most apparent expression of the new fashion. But fashion's formal and elegant character appeared already in the rich diversity of types of clothing designed for various times of day and purposes. The socially-involved lady had to have a wardrobe for morning, after-

noon, more and less formal evening occasions, street and rainwear, and various sports. Day clothing was made of sturdier woolen fabrics, complemented by coloured accessories, and was worn to cafes, cinemas, restaurants, and on visits to friends. Afternoon clothing was a very important part of the wardrobe. It was worn for afternoon socializing, having tea, on visits to friends, and for receiving guests at home. Such afternoon clothing was made of fine woolen or silk fabric, and was worn with a coat with fur or a fur jacket. In evening wear fashion made a very precise distinction between more and less formal occasions. More formal evening toilettes with decollete and without sleeves, reaching to the ground or even with a train, were reserved for dancing balls, theatre premieres, and receptions. They had to be complemented by an evening

Eva Pán a dáma na podzim 1931

"Gentleman and lady in autumn 1931", Eva, October 15th, 1931

Módní desatero *pro jaro 1930*

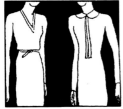

1. *Pás pevně utažený v pase; pokud jsou šaty bez pasu, přiléhají těsně k tělu a označují těsně pás nad boky.*

2. *Délka sukní se řídí podle denní doby a příležitosti: sportovní oblek pod kolena, cestovní oblek 38 centimetrů nad zemí, městský vycházkový oblek 34 centimetry nad zemí, odpolední společenský oblek 25 centimetrů nad zemí, večerní toaleta až ke kotníkům, plesová toaleta až k zemi.*

3. *Okraj sukně je stejně dlouhý pro všechny obleky vyjma plesové toalety, které mohou být vzadu delší, prodlouženy do vlečky.*

4. *Sukně jsou přiléhavé přes boky a rozšiřují se nad koleny v sežehlené záhyby u kostymů a sportovních šatů, v široké serpentiny u odpoledních a večerních šatů.*

5. *Bluza se nosí jen do sukně, podkasaná a přepásaná pasem. Anglická bluza není podmínkou: má i francouzský střih s ozdobou jaboту, knoflíčků, volánů, a tvoří někdy se sukní celkový oblek.*

6. *Anglické kostymy ovládnou na jaře ulici.*

7. *Plášť u ensemblu je buď dlouhý nebo tříčtvrteční. Oblíbený jest plášť rovný bez zvonu, ale doplněný pelerinkou dlouhou do půli zad.*

8. *Ozdobu šatů tvoří sámky, ažury, plissované volány a jaboty, ozdobné pásy. Největší novinkou jsou bolera, která se šijí u tweedových šatů stejně jako u šatů odpoledních a večerních.*

9. *Látky: šantung, imprimé, žoržetdouble, pique-lavable. Barvy: modrá, černá, zelená v kombinacích: bílá-černá, hnědá-bílá, modrá-bílá, hnědá-beige, černá-zelená. Novinkou je sytě růžová barva, kterou přináší Patou, a tmavě vínová.*

10. *Klobouky slaměné: hlavy nízké a široké, střechy klopené u angl. facon, u odpoledních klobouků oblíbená forma holandských čepečků. V oblibě jsou exotické slámy.*

JARNÍ PŘEHLÍDKA MÓDY

Pařížské modelové domy pořádají již velké přehlídky svých jarních a letních modelů, a majitelky módních salonů pražských vypravují se do Paříže, aby odtamtud přivezly módní novinky. Paříž už rozhodla o tom, co se bude na jaře nosit, odhlasovala mnoho novinek a překvapení — tady je jejich přehled.

Velkou módní novinkou jsou krátké pelerinky a bolera u všech druhů obleků, u plášťů, kostymů, odpoledních i večerních šatů. Šaty zůstávají přiléhavé a v pase přepásané, ale přes přiléhavý živůtek se obléká nebo je našit krátký kabátek nad pas nebo límec tak široký, že splývá skoro k pasu a tvoří pelerinku. U obleků z anglických látek je tento doplněk z téhož materiálu, u hedvábných šatů bývá z odlišného materiálu, krajky, tylu, georgettu a p.

Velkou péči věnuje jarní móda rukávům. Zavádí se opět rukávy krátké nebo tříčtvrteční, a uplatňují se na odpoledních šatech a na bluzách doplňujících kostymy. Na některých modelech jarních šatů objevují se dokonce rukávy od ramene k lokti rozšířené a pod loktem přiléhavé, nebo naopak rukávy k lokti přiléhavé a odtud se rozšiřující v serpentinový široký volán, volně splývající.

Na ulici se budou stále ještě nosit anglické kostymy smokingového střihu, nejoblíbenější bude pánská šedočerná látka s vlasem. Vedle těchto kostymů se budou nosit nejvíce tweedové komplety — tříčtvrteční plášť zdobený kožišinovým límcem a pod ním šaty z téhož materiálu, anglického střihu, zdobené bílým límečkem a manžetami.

Z barev si jarní móda vybrala prudce růžovou, tu které u nás říkáme „pouťová“, jedovatě zelenou, všechny pastelové barvy vedle černé, modré a bílé. Protože každá sezona musí být charakterisována určitou oblíbenou barvou, bude mít i tato jarní sezona svou zvláštní barvu — vínovou, tmavou červeně-fialovou barvu na kostymech, pláštích, odpoledních šatech, zkrátka na všem.

Imprimé georgetty, krepdešíny a šifony zůstávají od loňského roku velkou módou pro pozdější jaro a léto na šaty i kostymy. Objevují se ovšem docela nové barvy a vzory, loňské vzory platí již za zcela nemoderní, a největší módou budou vzory stříkané a mramorované bez určitých geometrických tvarů. Šaty z imprimé látky budou doplňovány plášti a krátkými kabátky pouze jednobarevnými.

Moiré a taft se přestává nosit, za to dochází velké obliby surové hedvábí pro letní šaty i kostymy, a prací nebo hedvábný pik na doplňky, límečky, manžety, knoflíčky, i celé bluzy a vestičky do kostymů.

Doplňkům obleků, kabelkám, šperkům, střevícům, punčochám, rukavicím se věnuje velká péče. Kabelku předpisuje móda z téhož materiálu jako oblek, ať je to tweed, krepdešín nebo imprimé. Ve špercích vedle spousty nevkusných barbarských ozdob jsou novinkou korále imprimé, totiž kuličky potažené látkou šatů. K hedvábným šatům se nosí punčochy stínované po délce nohy v několika odstínech hnědé, v šedé přecházející až do černa nebo modra a p. Rukavice se nosí dlouhé někdy až k lokti z jemné švédské kůže šedé, žluté, drapové, světle-hnědé. Kostymy a pláště jsou zdobeny umělou květinou v knoflíkové dírce, která se podle poslední módy z žíní. I večerní toalety jsou zdobeny velkými žíněnými květinami.

Jarní klobouky jsou vesměs slaměné, a to jen z drahých pletiv, manilla, panama, florentin atd. K letním imprimé šatům a kompletům budou se nosit širokánské klobouky až 60 cm v průměru. I jarní klobouky jsou skoro všechny širší formy.

Celkový ráz módy pro jaro a léto je: jednoduchost jen na vycházkovém a sportovním obleku, anglická móda jen pro sport a pro ulici, pro všechny ostatní příležitosti móda složitá, nákladná a zdůrazňující všechny detaily, plná ozdob a parády.

St. J.

coat, cape, or jacket. Less formal evening toilettes were used for all other occasions, such as the theatre, concerts, evening socializing, and entertainment. Such less formal wear was longer than afternoon clothing, reaching as low as the ankles, and always had sleeves and a small decollete. Convention permitted the wearing of a day coat with appropriate hat over less formal dress.

A garment suitable for the whole day besides evening occasions was the costume. However, even the costume had to have its qualities. A fashion reporter for *Eva* magazine, Staša Jilovská, recommended that well-off women acquire a costume as the basis for their entire wardrobe. A woman with little money should at least acquire the best costume and accessories as her only outfit. Jilovská maintained that it was better to have one perfect outfit with all accessories, rather than several of poor quality material and perpetually suffer lack of hats, shoes, and bags.[90]

Costumes were appropriate for work, for which women also needed special clothing. Work clothes should be simple, tasteful, should make an orderly but not eccentric appearance. Such clothing could be simple English garments of tweed, crepe, without unnecessary decoration and "extravagance". A woman had to have several such outfits for changing, and therefore they should not be expensive, ideally ready-made.[91]

"Gentleman and lady in autumn 1931", Eva, October 15th, 1931

Sports clothing for tennis, skiing, and other winter sports, for swimming and the beach, as well as cars and motorcycles, comprise a special section. Despite the strict distinction between specific kinds of clothing, throughout the 1930s there was a call for modesty in dress. In the period of the economic crisis, modesty was an economic necessity for most people, and even a fashion in the circles of high society. Helena Sedláková in *Eva* reported on the manner of dress in the summer season in Biarritz, where an almost snobbish rejection of social ceremony was in evidence. "A person who wears more than is permitted by the sport genre has ceased to be en vogue". Neither afternoon nor evening toilette, neither coattails nor dinner jackets were worn.[92]

In the Czech lands, where nine-tenths of the women had to skimp and save, modesty was caused by economic reasons rather than snobbism. Fashion reporters called for a deliberate approach to acquiring a dress. Staša Jilovská, for example, at the end of her report on Paris fashion news, discouraged her readers from purchasing evening wear: "Evening wear must be perfect, or should not exist at all. A perfect gown costs a lot, and a bad one is worse than nothing. No matter whether it's perfect or bad, it is nowadays a useless luxury. So think about it again!".[93]

Fashion rules for the spring of 1930, Eva, March 1st, 1930

Vkusné kalhotové a sukňové kombinace

Č. V 1124. Sukňová kombinace pod průsvitné šaty, dlouhá jako šaty. Živůtek má střih i tvar podprsenky a je lemován páskem z dvojitého tylu, v barvě látky. Střih vel. I.–II., spotřeba: 2 m látky, 70 cm široké.

Č. V 1125. Kalhotová bílá kombinace s podprsenkou připnutou páskem na knoflík. Je zdobena bleděmodrými lemy připojenými šitou ažurou. Střih vel. I.–II., spotřeba: 1·75 m l., 70 cm šir.

Č. V 1126. Kalhotová kombinace z krepdešínu je ozdobena aplikovanými pásky v tmavším odstínu téže látky. Kraje jsou začištěny šitou ažurou. Střih vel. II. je na příloze, spotřeba: 1·75 m světlé látky a 50 cm tmavší, 70 cm široké.

Č. V 1127. Přiléhavá kombinace pod odpolední šaty je šita z lesklého saténu. Podprsenkový živůtek je z růžové látky. Střih vel. II. je na příloze. Spotřeba: 2·30 m látky, 70 cm široké.

Č. V 1128. Krátká hedvábná košilka zdobena aplikací lesklého saténu. Střih vel. 0.–I., spotřeba: 1·80 m látky, 70 cm široké.

Č. V 1129. Bílá kalhotová kombinace zdobená našívanými pracími stuhami z hedvábí, modrými a růžovými. Střih vel. I.–II., spotřeba: 1·80 m základní látky a 50 cm barevné, 70 cm široké.

Underwear, Vkus, July 1931

ELEGANCI
ŠTÍHLOST
KRÁSU

našimi korselety
„Odip" PRAHA II.,
Myslíkova ul. 15.
Továrna: Bubeneč, Uralské nám. 447.

Eva 1.1.1933

SOCHOR

SOCHOROVY
TEXTILNÍ
ZÁVODY
VE DVOŘE KRÁLOVÉ n. L.
PRÁVĚ ZAHÁJILY VÝROBU
PRAVÉHO PŘÍRODNÍHO
HEDVÁBÍ
JAKO PRVNÍ VÝTVOR
OHLAŠUJÍ VÁM SVŮJ
CRÊPE DE CHINE
SOCHOR,
ČISTÉ PŘÍRODNÍ HEDVÁBÍ
ZARUČENÉ STÁLOBAREVNÉ.

É HEDVÁBNÉHO CRÊPE DE CHINE SOCHOR.

Design by the UREUS fashion house,
Prague II, Rokoko-Lucerna, Eva,
February 15th, 1931

Chat Noir
EAU DE COLOGNE

splývá s přirozenou vůní pleti
a dodává jí fascinující vůně...

Furthermore, in the Czech lands of the 1920s the reserved attitude to decorative style of dress and to useless fashion changes was still felt. The characteristic most valued in clothing was the quality of the material and cut, while fashionability was only valued up to the point that it started drawing attention to the wearer. This is why the English style of dress was so valued in Czechoslovakia; it was practical, elegant, and did not submit to frequent changes.

The real relationship of Prague ladies from intellectual and business circles to fashion was apparent from a poll published by *Eva* magazine in season

fashions only out of fear of appearing eccentric. They only chose the simplest and most modest designs. They preferred an English outfit which replaced a number of other useless outfits. "Simplicity and tastefulness wins over the excesses of fashion".[94]

The ideal woman of the beginning of the 1930s had a slim, lithe athletic figure. Though the figure was no longer boyish, it did not feature a pronounced bust, waist, and hips. Underwear, which helped to create this figure, was a rubber garter belt and shaped bra or elastic rubber corset connected with a lace or silk bra which supported the body without deforming it. Other parts of ladies' underwear were short, bell-shaped panties and trouser or skirt slips.

A remarkable feature of the new fashion was the shape of the skirt. It was lengthened, narrow at the hips, and flared below them. The cut could be straight with inset folds, backstitched at the top, and loose at the bottom. The cut could alternately feature inset pleated sections twisting around the hips, with variously designed yokes or tunics.

Imprimé bude case v létě velkou módou. Má nové vzory, drobné tečky a kytičky, a šijí se z něho lehké lázeňské šaty i kostymy.

Summer imprimé dress, drawing by V. Michal, Eva , April 1st, 1929,

of 1930 — 31. Answers to the questions — 1. How many suits do you have? 2. What kinds are they? 3. For what purpose are they? 4. Which one do you like the most? 5. Why that particular one and not another? — ranged between the curt "I most like the suit which has a clean collar at the moment" and a wardrobe consisting of two or three suits of a certain kind. A summary of the results of this poll was in accord with the views of fashion reporters: Czech women submitted to new

Evening outfit — dress and cape of yellow-green printed voil-chiffon interwoven with gold thread, decorated with fur, Rosenbaum, Prague, around 1930, M. D. A., inv.no. 72.569

Negligé, sewn by B. Zvárová, a tailor of the Rosenbaum fashion house, Prague 1930, M. D. A., inv. no. 88.658

Fialové georgettové se zakládanými sámky a přeštepovanými (jako hol-faldičky) vždy proti sobě, dole roz-puštěné. Na živůtku jsou figury vrchem nakládané a hodně v krajíčku vyštepo-vané. Střevíčky v téže barvě a mat.

Bledémodro-stříbrné brokátové (měkký brokát), límec u cape z polární lišky, perlová čelenka, též šperk z perliček. Střevíčky z téhož brokátu.

Chiffonový oblek, k tomu krátká same-tová jupička. Límec a rukávy zdobené když jsou

vkládané šnůrky, ale je to docíleno jen trochu širším sámkem na stojato vyžehleným ze spodu).

Dívčí šatečky z bílého tylu opásané širokou bledémodrou stuhou (růžové kytičky), že dojem je takřka již empírový. Holfaldy na sukni trochu dole do široka. Rukávečky z jedno-duché látky jen lem dvojitý.

Růžové chiffonové (nebo imprimé) s malou pláštěnkou, ovšem všitou u výstřihu. Serpentinové volány se sbíhají napřed do drobného plissé.

Evening toilettes, drawings by H. Vlková, Eva, November 1st, 1929

Around the middle of the decade the skirt was widened with a slit. Another feature of fashion in the 1930s, which in the 1920s Madame Vionet had applied on her designs, was a bias cut. Dresses that were diagonally cut best met the demands of fashion of the 1930s, lightly hugging the body and flowing down in gentle folds, creating natural, shallow bells. They were so flexible that they did not require buttoning at the waist. The diagonal cut was also used in evening and day wear. The 1930s were the golden age of formal evening wear. Cuts of less formal evening and dancing ball toilettes were not in fact different from one another. Ball gowns were characterized by substantial decolletes at the back that reached almost to the waist, and a skirt that reached to the ground and often extended into a short train. Besides the sheath cut with narrow skirt at the hips, enlarged into a bell-

Evening outfit – dress and jacket of beige lace and beige georgette, the Schiller fashion house, Prague, around 1930, M. D. A., inv. no. 72.601

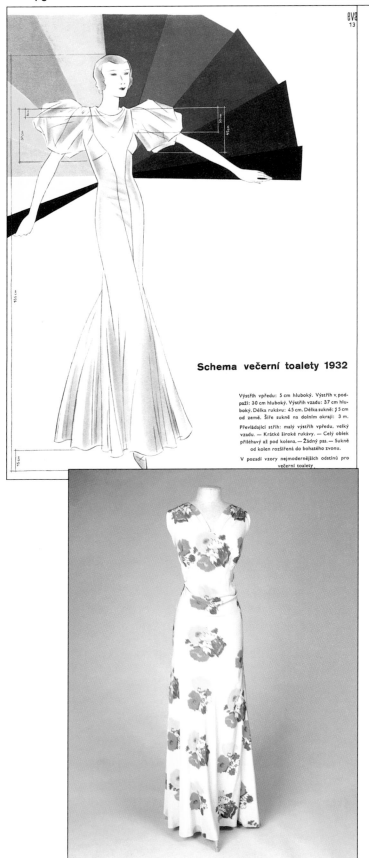

Schema večerní toalety 1932

Výstřih vpředu: 5 cm hluboký. Výstřih v. pod-
paží: 30 cm hluboký. Výstřih vzadu: 37 cm hluboký. Délka rukávu: 45 cm. Délka sukně: 5 cm
od země. Šíře sukně na dolním okraji: 3 m.
Převládající střih: malý výstřih vpředu, velký
vzadu. — Krátké široké rukávy. — Celý oblek
přiléhavý až pod kolena. — Žádný pas. — Sukně
od kolen rozšířená do bohatého zvonu.

V pozadí vzory nejmodernějších odstínů pro
večerní toalety.

Summer evening toilette of white imprimé taffeta,
Rosenbaum, Prague 1933, M. D. A., inv.no. 72.570

Evening toilette
1932, Eva,
November 1st,
1932

shape from knees down, a kind of stylish dress
with wide skirt was still current. At the beginning
of the 1930s, the formal evening gown was cut
and belted at or slightly above the waistline, and
was folded at the back. In 1932 fashion magazines recommended a dress with princess cut
that was unbroken at the waist. Necklines grew
somewhat smaller. Artificial flowers, ribbons,
fringes were attached to the shoulders. Informal
evening dresses appeared with elaborately designed sleeves. It was fashionable to combine
two kinds of material: shiny with matte fabrics,
heavy with light material, black with white or other
soft shaded fabric. A recommended accessory
was a short evening coat. Somewhat later —
around 1934 — the cuts of dresses remained the
same, but used heavier materials, primarily velvet
and velour-chiffon. Short evening covers were
worn with the dresses. A short pelerine of tulle
furbelows was especially admired. In 1935 *Eva*
magazine introduced several new hits: soft flowing folds on skirt and bodice inspired by ancient
draperies. In Paris, Mme Grès used them the most
in his designs. Another hit were "midnight outfits" — two-piece formal gowns with long skirts
and a dinner or other type jacket. At the same
time, a new type of formal wear also appeared
that was designed for meetings with friends between afternoon and evening — "robes de cock-
tails". They were characterized by skirts that were longer than on afternoon dresses, and
decolletes. Tight-fitting narrow dresses that were
widened, either with folding set into the middle
of the front piece or a back piece arranged to resemble a bustle, still remained in fashion.

The first signs of significant changes appeared in
reports from Parisian fashion shows in autumn
1936. Tunics were again used in formal and informal wear, and the influence of the Directoire and
Redingot, with tight-fitting bodices and high, pronounced breasts, was apparent. Besides formal
suits with long skirts, outfits with short skirts
made of decorative materials like lamé and brocade started to assert themselves. Formal types
of tunics could be complemented by trousers
of light materials as well as by skirts.

The cuts of walking and afternoon dresses developed in the same manner as formal evening
gowns. At the beginning of the 1930s, the dresses
were cut at the waist and belted. Around 1932,

Less formal evening outfit, black
wool, Marthe Loeff, Prague,
around 1933, M. D. A.,
inv.no. 85.357

From the wedding of
Viktor Podolský
and Věra Černá,
Eva, October 1st, 1935

▲ Obrázek ze svatební hostiny. Od leva do prava
pí Hilda Podolská, p. Zika Ascher, sl. Majda Hra-
bánková, p. Jirka Grégr, sl. Hanka Ledererová,
ženich Viktor Podolski, nevěsta Věra Podolská,
JUDr. Karel Šulc, sl. Slávka Letzová.

Nevěsta v objetí
přítelkyň: sl. Le-
dererová (vlevo),
nevěsta, sl. Hra-
bánková.

▲ FOTO CAROLA
Jako z knihy pohádek. Ne-
věsta, paní Věra Podolská,
v těsném bílém hedvábí
a záplavě jemného tylu.

Jeden z mnoha připitků.
Veden od leva
slečnou Ledererovou, p. V.
Hrabánkem, slečnou Letzovou, p. Milošem
Podolskim a jeho paní, Hildou Podolskou.
FOTO HÁJEK ▼

│ Chvilka oddechu a důvěrného rozho-
▼ voru před rozloučením.

CHCETE BÝT HOSTY

na svatební hostině?

...u v Praze události, ba skoro
...ostí. Paní Hanna Podolská vy-
...o syna, p. Viktora Podolského
...sl. Věru Černou, krásnou
...a nejen rodinnou a společen-
...přehlídkou elegantních toalet.

Evening toilette of black and white satin, Prague, around 1933, M. D. A., inv. no. 82.412
Evenig outfits, Rosenbaum, Prague, around 1935, M. D. A., inv. no. 87.568, 86.438

Evening toilette, Marthe Loeff, Prague. Eva, December 1st, 1934 ►

Atelier Club

Evening outfit — dress with jacket of black silk and tulle, Rosenbaum, Prague,
Eva, November 1st, 1936

Šedý kostym kombinovaný ze tří
nů šedé barvy. Kabát má třičtvr
rukávy, halenka je nejsvětlejšího
s dlouhými přilehavými rukávy, uj
zdobená červenou úzkou šále

Anglický kostym s třičtvrtečním kabátem z vroubk
látky. Sukně je z hladké látky téže barvy, halenka
tého jerseye.

Vycházkové šaty z beige vlněné látky, doplněné pelerin
která se zapíná vzadu u krku, takže se mohou šaty nosit i b
jsou zdobeny sámky a lemy z bílé vlněné látky.

Vycházkové šaty z tmavěšedé vlněné látky, doplněné pelerinkou,
je vzadu u krku přišita, jinak volně splývá přes ramena. Ozdoba
lého hrubého hedvábí.

"Dress for walking", Eva, March 15th, 1933

simple sleeves became more elaborate. Almost at
the same time, a kimono cut, waisted with a belt
or horizontally folded piece of cloth, became fashionable. Dresses complemented by pelerines or
pelerine collars made from the same cloth as the
dress itself were also favoured.

Practical and elegant suits of all kinds — dress
with overcoat, dress with jacket or pelerine —
remained in style throughout the 1930s. Jackets
could be short or three-quarter length and have
a straight cut or bell-shaped cut widened into the
shape of a paletot. After ten years, cossack jackets
once again came into fashion. An informal suit
consisting of an English woolen skirt, blouse, and
knitted vest, or a skirt with pullover, was favored
for walking, sports, or work. Thanks to its practicality, knitwear found application in 1930s fashion
in all forms: as vests instead of jackets, pullovers
instead of blouses, sport sweaters, bathing suits,
caps, wrappers, gloves, socks and kneehighs, as
well as for entire dresses and outfits.

Mrs. Hilda Podolská in evening toilette from the fashion house
Podolská, Prague, around 1936, photographed by Carola

První vlaštovky se
objevují na francouzské
Rivieře -

*Společenská
odpoledne*

KRESLILA H. VLKOVÁ

Odpolední šaty ze světle zelené rosalby mají živůtek vpředu zdobený dvěma pruhy látky, které pře-
cházejí z řasení v výstřihu rovně až po celé délce
sukně, která je pod nimi skládaná. Kimonové rukávy se od lokte rozšiřují a jsou v zápěstí sepjaty
úzkou manžetou. Pás je sřasený z téže látky.

Fislové šaty z hustého krepovaného georgettu, celé
jednobarevné, zdobené jen drobnými ručními sámky,
které probíhají kolmo po celém živůtku až přes boky,
odkud je sukně hladká.

Jednoduché šaty bez ozdob odlišné barvy platí letos
za nejelegantnější.

...komplet z řídké vlněné látky.
... přepásané černým koženým pa-
...ou sponou, a niklovými knoflíky.
...en černým persiánovým límcem.
...né.

...ostym z drobně kostičkové látky
..., zdobený úzkými záložkami šik-
...mo setízenými. Je doplněn raglánovým plá-
štěm z téže látky, s černými doplňky.

Černošedý komplet: kostym je z šedé látky
...

Afternoon dress, drawing by H. Vlková,
Eva, October 1st, 1935

Spring outfits and costumes, drawing
by H. Vlková, Eva, February 1st, 1932

Afternoon dress with bolero. Outfit
for walking — dress and paletot,
Rosenbaum, Prague, around 1933,
M. D. A., inv. no. 76.015, 86.774

Summer garments had similar character. Formal wear was made of imprimé fabric — printed natural silk such as crepe-de-Chine, or chiffon — or of artificial silk, which was favoured for its low price and durability. In 1934 the Sochor company introduced non-creasing artificial silk called Sotila (a shortening of Sochorova tiskárna látek — The Sochor Fabric Printing Company).[95] The next year the company introduced an improved material called Sonora. A simple dress of single-coloured cloth and simple cut, with minute decorative details such as decorative buttoning, pockets, embroidered emblems, and coloured texture, was meant for summer days in the city and country. Outfits consisting of bathing suits, bodices with various kinds of shoulder straps, beach skirts, and buttoned dresses, short and long trousers, which could be combined in numerous manners and variations, were designed for the water. Throughout the 1930s beach pyjamas remained in favour, and sometimes

Prací šaty pro teplé dny na venku

Bílé plátěné šaty zdobené červeným a zeleným stepováním z pracího hedvábí. Pás z bílé kůže.

Modré plátěné šaty zdobené bíločervenou proužkovanou lístkou. Pás z červené matné kůže.

Šaty z krémového, uzlíčkovitě tkaného plátna. Pás z pestře pruhovaného plátna též kvality. Monogram je prostepován a podložen vlnou, aby plasticky vystupoval.

Bílé šaty z látky modročervené tečkované. Kravata také z plátna. Pás z modré kůže.

KRESLILA H. VLKOV

"Summer outfits for hot da
the country", drawir
H. Vlková, Eva, June 15th, 1

were even recognized as formal evening wear. The political situation in Central Europe in the mid 1930s and the resulting patriotic mood provoked another period of folkloristic fashion among Czech women. In 1936, the Sochor textile company, in cooperation with the Melantrich studio, reacted to the world fashion of summer dresses that resembled German dirndels by creating a series of cotton fabrics for summer dresses with patterns inspired by folk ornamentation in the national colours, red, white, and blue. They were called šohajka or, for the foreign market, Slovanka.[66] The distinctive line of the Sochor textile company was in later years expanded with a number of new styles and patterns, such as a scarf fabric called Milena. The Czech public accepted "svéráz" fabrics with great excitement and incorporated them not only in women's summer wardrobes, but also in uniforms for political celebrations and rallies. Their production continued until the beginning of the Second World War when the company was changed to war production.[97]

Spring overcoats, drawing by B. Vavrečková, Měsíc, June 1932

eva
1. června 1933
ročník V. číslo 15

Track-suit, Eva, June 1st, 1933

Šohajky

Summer dress with
folkloristic
patterns, Eva,
April 1st, 1936

I
štíhl...
z nás...
radil...
dá vy...
jsem s...
obchodn...
u Baro...
skvostný...
dva model...
nakresliti...
z vlny s l...
tištěný vkus...
barevným vzus...
plavky od Ba...
stavují dokon...

Swimming outfit, the J. Baron company, Prague,
Jungmann square no. 1, Eva, June 15th, 1937

ᵉᵛᵃ Na sluníčku a na písku
16

u moře oblékněte si pyjama podle ně-
kterého z našich vzorků. Je to oblek,
který vám nahradí v lázních mnoho
drahých šatů, a oblíbíte si jej pro jeho
slušivost a pohodlnost.

Kreslil V. Michal

Eva 1.5.1938

Beach pyjama,
drawing by V. Michal,
Eva, June 15th, 1931

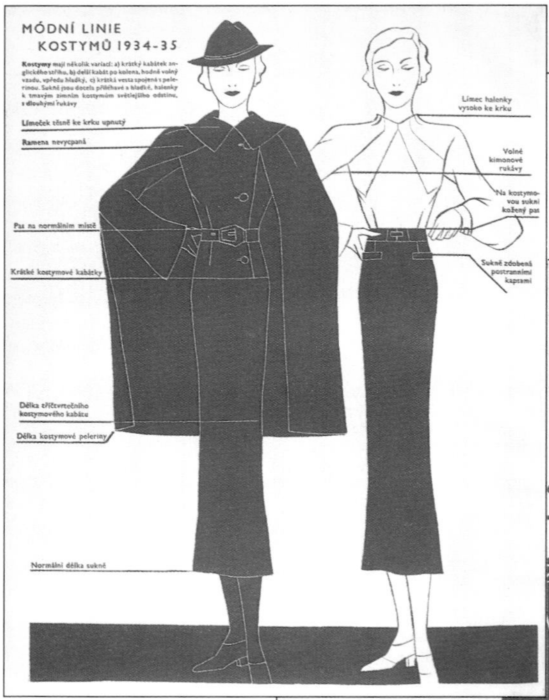

MÓDNÍ LINIE KOSTYMŮ 1934-35

Kostymy mají několik variací: a) krátký kabátek anglického střihu, b) delší kabát po kolena, hodně volný vzadu, vpředu hladký, c) krátká vesta spojená s pelerínou. Sukně jsou docela přiléhavé a hladké, buď k tmavým jinoon kostymovém svétlejšího odstínu, s dlouhými rukávy.

Limček těsně ke krku upnutý

Ramena nevycpaná

Pas na normálním místě

Krátké kostymové kabátky

Délka tříčtvrtečního kostymového kabátu

Délka kostymové peleriny

Normální délka sukně

Límec halenky vysoko ke krku

Volné kimonové rukávy

Na kostymovou sukni kožený pas

Sukně zdobená postranními kapsami

Fashion line 1934 — 35,
Eva, October 1st, 1934

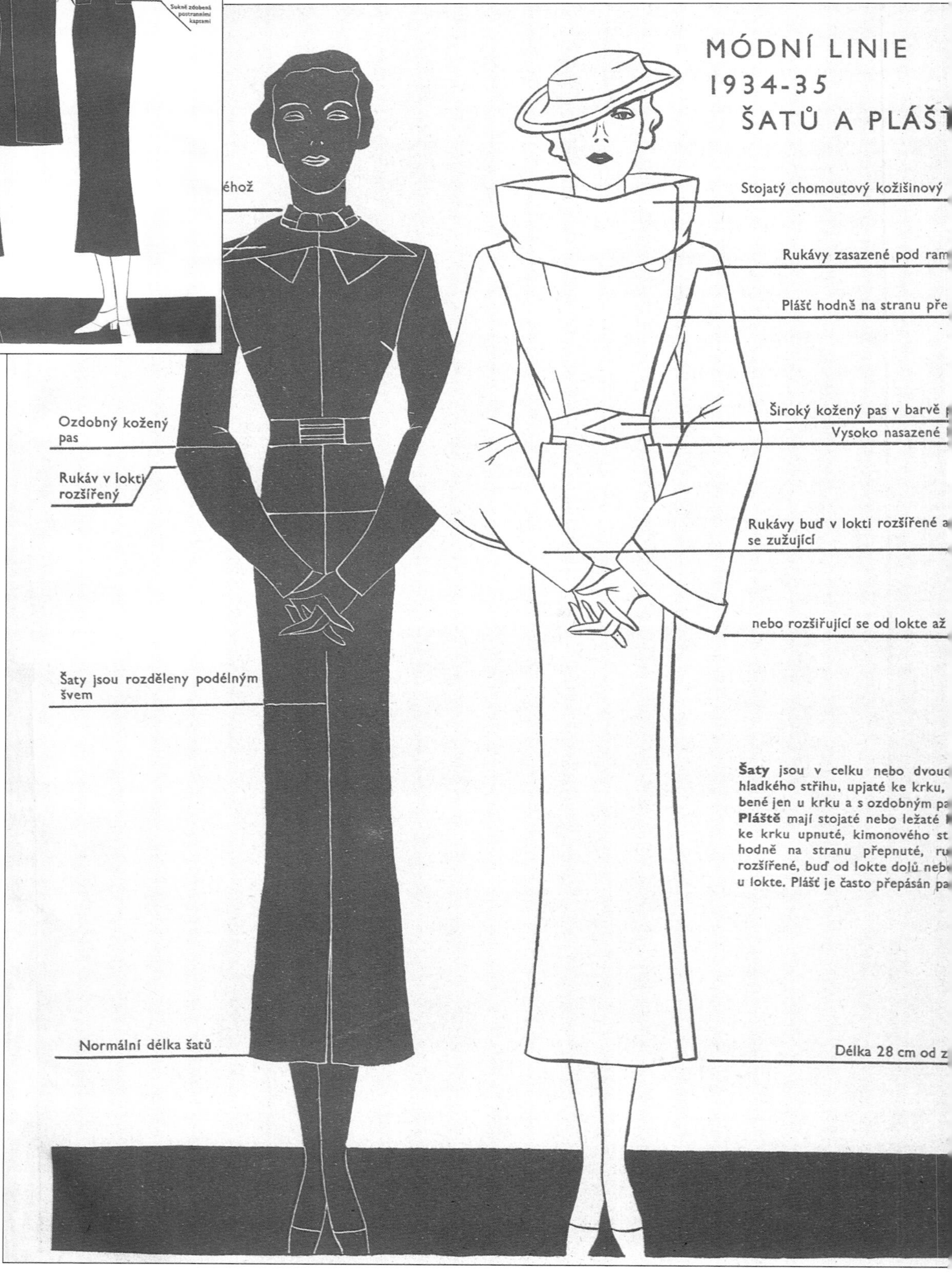

MÓDNÍ LINIE 1934-35 ŠATŮ A PLÁŠŤ

Stojatý chomoutový kožišinový

Rukávy zasazené pod ram

Plášť hodně na stranu pře

Široký kožený pas v barvě

Vysoko nasazené

Rukávy buď v lokti rozšířené a se zužující

nebo rozšiřující se od lokte až

...éhož

Ozdobný kožený pas

Rukáv v lokti rozšířený

Šaty jsou rozděleny podélným švem

Šaty jsou v celku nebo dvouc
hladkého střihu, upjaté ke krku,
bené jen u krku a s ozdobným pa
Pláště mají stojaté nebo ležaté
ke krku upnuté, kimonového st
hodně na stranu přepnuté, ru
rozšířené, buď od lokte dolů neb
u lokte. Plášť je často přepásán pa

Normální délka šatů

Délka 28 cm od z

Outfits were still either tailor made in the English style, or were made in the French style with a decoratively designed jacket. The dinner jacket with long lapels and closed with a single button remained popular. The popularity of "cossack" tunics, in which a narrow costume skirt was complemented by a three-quarter length jacket widened into a bell shape, spread in the middle of the 1930s. In the same period, French costumes also slightly changed: they featured protruding tails or folds at the back. They could also have longer, so-called "swallow", round tails as on a frock-coat. Winter outfits were richly adorned with short-hair fur. Alternatives to outfits were dresses or skirts complemented by paletots of a more or less widened shape, which often replaced even overcoats.

Overcoats of the early 1930s continued in the same style as at the end of the previous decade. They were straight, moderately tight-fitting, with the two front pieces wrapped over each other, buttoned at one side. High collars, decorated with fur, were shortened over the course of time until they lay smoothly on the shoulders or were entirely replaced by a collar in the shape of a shawl. For the Central European spring and autumn, ladies were recommended to wear a kind of man's trench coat with warm lining, an ulster coat in brown, blue, or grey colours, or a raglan coat of gaberdine with lining. For rainy days, a waterproof coat of impregnated silk or rubber, fitted with a high collar or hood and deep patch pockets, was appropriate.

Sport clothing of this period did not differ from that of the 1920s. An outfit of Norwegian type was worn for skiing, but was increasingly replaced by a waterproof windbreaker. Wide, long Norwegian trousers were shortened to resemble knickers, but towards the end of the 1930s again were lengthened and narrowed into the form of ski pants of the postwar period. Trouser skirts were still recommended for winter sport outfits, and long flannel trousers were

recommended for hiking and trips to the country.

For nature sports, however, even more suitable was a new hit: a track suit consisting of long trousers and tucked up jacket of woolen tricot. For tennis a simple white summer dress was worn; but during the 1930s long or short trousers asserted themselves even for ladies. Over the years, bathing suits acquired an underwear-type cut, with formed cut at the bosom. Two-piece swimming and sunbathing suits started to be used. They were made of woolen jersey or, at the end of the decade, of lastex — material stitched with rubber threads.

Raincoats, drawing by
the Lopae studio, Eva,
February 15th, 1932

Kožišiny na nových podzimních modelech

Č. V 1316. Hnědý plášť z vlněné látky zdobený kožišinou z leoparda, má moderní postavený tvar límce, vybíhající v revery. Pas z látky, prostepovaný, má velkou dřevěnou sponu v barvě kožišiny. Střih vel. I.–II. Spotřeba: 3 m látky, 130 cm široké.

Č. V 1317. Mladistvý kostym ze šedé, uzlovitě tkané látky fresko, je zdoben šedým persiánem na límci a manžetách. Knoflíky šedé, dřevěné. Nosí se do něj barevné halenky. Střih vel. II. je napříloze. Spotřeba: 3 m látky, 130 cm široké.

Č. V 1318. Béžový vlněný plášť se širokými revery je zdoben tmavě hnědým persiánem. Zapínání je dvouřadové, na knoflíky v barvě kožišiny. Rukávy jsou ozdobně prostepované. Střih vel. II.–III. Spotřeba: 3·25 m látky, 130 cm široké.

Č. V 1319. Červený plášť, francouzského střihu je zdoben límcem a lemy z hnědé tulení kožišiny. Široké revery jsou zvonovitě rozšířené a výborně sluší postavám v prsou slabým. Střih vel. 0.–I. Spotřeba: 3·25 m látky, 130 cm široké.

Autumn overcoats, drawing
by M. Kučerovská, Vkus,
August 1934

FOTO BARTOŇ

KABELKY

Z EVINY VITRINKY

Výkladní skříně se na jaře vyznačují vždy největší zajímavostí, ale letos jsou trumfem kabelky. Kabelka — předmět, který nás ani na krok neopouští, který trpělivě snáší vše co do něj nacpeme a kterého si přes to nevšímáme, jest náhle středem pozornosti. A právem – kdo by mohl macešsky zacházet s kabelkou, plochou jako kniha, potaženou tmavomodrou jelenicí se sametovým dotykem, a jejíž vnitřek jest zařízen tak, že každý předmět, pudřenka, rtěnka, peněženka, notes i plnicí pero má svou přihrádku, a kabelka jest vždy jako uklizená. Podobná, ale mnohem menší jest kabelka z černého krokodíla, je určená výhradně pro odpoledne nebo večer a skryjete v ní jen nejnutnější zkrašlovací utensilie. Začatý pullover, dopisy a vzorky látek na nový kostym musíme rozhodně nechat doma. Jiný druh kabelek jest z úžasně měkké kůže, zpracované jako látka. Kůže se u závěru nabírá, vrapuje a i prošívá různými, vatou podloženými ornamenty, držadla jsou mohutná a jakoby předimensovaná. Jiné mají opět fantastický tvar, jsou zdobené kolem zipového uzávěru plastickými, měkce plněnými válci a vyvolávají nadšení u všech žen nosících kabelky pod paží. Naše obrázky vám všechny popsané typy dobře znázorňují, cenu i nákupní pramen na dotaz vám sdělí redakce.

Kresba a montáž A. Langová.

eva
19

"Handbags from Eva's display case",
Eva, March 15th, 1936

Střízlivý střih, propracované detaily

Světle šedý tříčtvrteční kostym, který se hodí zvlášť pro vysoké štíhlé postavy. je doplněn šedomodrou halenkou, ostatní doplňky šedé. Drap anglický tailleur z lehké pánské látky smokingového střihu. Nosí se k němu měkký plstěný klobouk hnědý nebo drap, a světlá nebo hnědá halenka nebo pletený jumper.

Odpolední jarní plášť nejnovějšího střihu: charakteristické jsou tříčtvrteční široké rukávy a chomoutový límec, který si však mohou dovolit jen ženy s delším krkem.

Klasický raglánový plášť, vhodný do každého počasí a skoro ke každé příležitosti. Nosí se přes šaty nebo přes lehký jarní kostym.

kreslila H.

Nebudou to jen pelerinky, které budou p vládat na jarních ulicích. Stejně modern elegantní zůstává klasický kostym, ke k rému se vždycky rády vracíme, když n omrzí poslední novinky, a klasický pl raglánového střihu zůstane také vždy v ným naším přítelem. Kdo má na rozmyš nou mezi kostymem a pelerinkovým ko pletem, udělá vždy dobře, když zvolí k tym, který nepodléhá módě a je vhodn oblekem od jara do podzimu ku vše denním příležitostem. A jak je zapotř dobrého anglického pláště, poznaly jste jistě samy, když jste si uvědomily, že ani na jaře nesvítí po sluníčko a že i v květnu může přijít déšť a chladno. Šaty pod takový plášť jsou vždy barvou shodné, na p hnědé k beige plášti nebo naopak, zelené k hnědému, šedé, modré k šedému. Oblek zpestří barev doplňky. Šaty samy jsou docela hladké, rovné, přilehavé, s krátkými nebo tříčtvrtečními rukávy, s mal ozdobou u krku a širokým koženým pásem.

Látky přináší jaro zase nové a krásné, měkké lehké vlněné jerseye a veloury, látky kombinované z vl a hedvábí, s jemnými vzorky, v nichž převládá kostka. Kombinuje se vždy s látkou bez vzoru, jednobarevne

PŘÍJEMNÉ HODINY
NNÝCH DNŮ

Madame **TOMBO**

a vrátila z Paříže — *a Londýna*

a přivezla nové překrásné modely dámských klobouků.

Dovoluje

si Vás milostivá tímto pozvat k jeho přehlídce.

Modelový dům dámských klobouků.
Praha, Václavské nám. 12. ● **Tel. 38.207.** ● **Lift**

IK NA VEČERNÍCH ŠATECH

K bílé plátěné sukni nosí se kabátek s imprimé hedvábného plátna.

Také bílý pik může být zvarhovaný. Ušije pěkný dlouhý plášť se se... z hlazené rukavičkové kůž...

Tříčtvrteční paleto se vzor... plissovaná sukně a šála z ...

Elegantní kostym z čes... Sukně je plissovaná, boha...

Kreslila H. Vlková

...eznamená, že by se nosily ...o vyšívanými vykřičníky; ... vykřičník a střevíce pod ...chtěla přednášet na téma: ... nesociálního cítění mo... ... všechno to tedy nezna... ...ito ve smyslu: čím vykři...

...ých základních rysech se ...ty sezonně módními, jsou ...mnoho pozornosti látce. ...cítíte, že ať si ušijete šaty ...sametu. Jindy to je barva. ...? – jindy to je tvar, vzpo...

...výstřihy. Když si tak pro... ...cítíte najednou hlubokou ...lidé dovedou ty výstřihy

...letošní móda připravuje ...ci, co patří dopředu a co ...cený svět, když jsou šaty vpředu hole, rovné, bez ozdob a celá paráda vzadu – výstřihy, mašle, pérové ozdoby, květy a t. p.?

A abychom se k těm výstřihům vrátily. Tedy většinou jsou, jak už jsme řekly, na zádech. A nyní jejich variace: celá záda zůstávají nahá, jen proužek látky je kolem krku; záda nahá, ale přes ně křížem dva široké pruhy látky, takže z černé látky vykřikují čtyři růžové čtverce kůže; bohatě sřasený límec kolem krku a pod ním hluboká špička trojúhelníkového výstřihu; výstřihy elipsovité, čtvercové, obdélníkové, hvězdicovité. Prostě – uplatňují se tu všechny plošné útvary probírané i neprobírané v sextánské planimetrii. Opravdu lidská vynalézavost nezná hranic a kdyby tu neudaly hranice zákony o mravopočestnosti, závodily bychom letos na plesech ve svých výstřizích s pověstnými výstřihy krásné Salambo.

Protože dále není možno riskovat, aby všechen náš nebo švadlenin důvtip zůstal nepovšimnut, je nutno výstřihy, na něž se vyplýtvalo tolik fantasie, ještě nějak zdůraznit. A tak je potkáváte zdobené pery, krajkami, stuhou, sřasením látky, květy a t. p.

Než tímhle naše kapitola ještě nekončí. Když se móda rozhodla stříhat, tak stříhá. Když stříhá do životku, proč by si nemohla troufat také na sukni? Sukně u večerních šatů obepíná podle módního předpisu pevně boky a nohy ke kolenům. Dokonce u partii kolenou jsou letošní sukně tak úzké, že se obdivujete, jak se mohou ženy v těchto šatech vůbec pohybovat. První krok vám tajemství prozradí: Sukně je rozstřižena. A ne jenom na jednom místě, často i na více místech a obnažuje nohu až téměř ke kolenu.

Tento módní nápad se tak šmahem a rychle zalíbil, že ho teď ženy hodlají co nejvíce využít a zneužít. Tak rozstřihují sukně nejen večerních šatů, nýbrž i šatů pro odpoledne a dokonce potkáváte na ulicích i v kavárnách sukně, rozstřihané až po kolena na malé praporky, třepetající se kolem nohou, což je nevkusné, nemístné, nechutné, prostě – ne– ne– ne–.

A tak končím apelem:

Vážené výstřihy,

jste jistě velmi krásné a jak se odborně říká ‚velmi slušivé‘. Staly jste se nyní velmi populárními a to by mohlo být velkým, dokonce váš život ohrožujícím nebezpečím. Radím vám tedy: zůstaňte skromné, podržte si svou večerní půdu, která vám sluší a nenadýmejte se expansivními plány zabrat ještě odpoledne a dopoledne, protože by to mohlo znamenat váš konec.

V plné úctě Van.   Z. F. M.

Do společnosti

Odpolední šaty doplněny pláštěn... též látky, lemov... úzkými pruhy h... línu nebo j. kož...

Lyžařský kostym 1932
a jeho doplňky

Outfit for skiing 1932, drawing by Z. Fuchsová, Eva, December 1st, 1932

Summer overcoats and costumes, drawing by H. Vlková,
Eva, May 1st, 1936

Spring overcoats and costumes, drawing by H. Vlková, Eva, March 1st, 1935

Afternoon dress, drawing by Zd. Fuchsová, Eva, November 1st, 1934

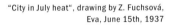

KRESLILA Z. M. F.

"City in July heat", drawing by Z. Fuchsová,
Eva, June 15th, 1937

eva

Eva 15. 5. 1937   Scheme of a fashion silhouette
in spring 1938, drawing
by Z. Fuchsová,
Eva, March 1st, 1938

Jiné domy pak přinášejí mnoho modelů, kde proti této dlouhé linii volí řešení příčné. Sem patří šaty, a bude jich asi mnoho, s krátkým bolerem a přestřihovanými živůtky (i dvakrát, nad pasem a pod pasem). Pro večer jsou nová zvonová paleta, která se převlékají přes hlavu a jsou bohatě zdobena korálky a výšivkami.

Mainbocher přináší docela nové modely, které označuje jako „československou módu". Zřejmě mu vzorem byly slovenské kroje. Jsou to halenky a odpolední i večerní šaty, jež jsou bohatě nabrané u krku i v pase, takže živůtek i sukně jsou bohatě zřazeny. I rukávy jsou nabrané.

Linie dlouhých plášťů je celkem neurčitá, spíše rovná. Ale jestliže vám spíše sluší střih řasnatý, pak si zvolte plášť s bohatým záhybem vzadu. Pásů je málo nebo jen poloviční.

Význačné jsou také letošní barevné kombinace, které mění celkový vzhled modelů. Tak se nosí velmi světlé kabátky k černé sukni, nebo imprimé zvonové pláště k jednobarevným šatům a podobně.

1939

ÁTKÁ ČI DLOUHÁ?

é pařížské domy propagují každý svou vlastní módní linii, kterou důsledně uplat-
delech pro den i večer. V celku však postihneme v letošních kolekcích asi dvojí
ěkteré domy přinášejí modely s prodlouženým pasem a vše co k prodloužení linie
opagují tedy delší kostymové kabátky, často se zakulacenými šosy, nebo i tunikové
pínané dvouřadově, na 8–10 knoflíků. Podobně řešeny jsou i šaty, jejichž živůtek
polou boků, takže připomínají silně tuniky. Jejich sukně jsou často skládané (od
ku), a záhyby jsou rozžehlené. Halenky do pasu dosluhují, většina halenek se nosí
často prodloužené až do polou boků. Tuto linii sledují i velmi jednoduché, hladké
áště.
:harakteristická je i volba materiálu, záplava proužkovaných látek, položených
že také zdůrazňují prodloužení linie.

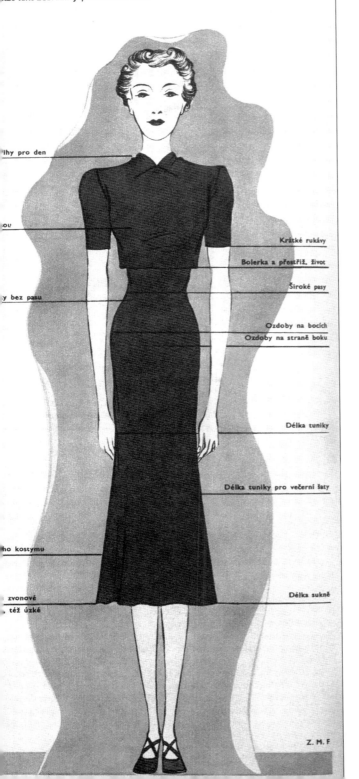

Women's clothing at the end of the 1930s was analogous to the pre-war political situation in Europe, which was marked by naive optimism and, at the same time, by realistic preparation for war. On the one hand, fashion introduced a number of practical elements marking the suffering of war and a style that came from men's clothing; on the other hand, fashion asserted a new ideal of feminine beauty based on the "natural line" of the full bosom, slim waist and round hips, complemented by a straight back, wide shoulders, and upright figure. Together with this new ideal of the feminine figure, signs of a more feminine sense of fashion returned: long hair, arranged into complicated hair styles, short and wider skirts, folding, flounces, fichu and, of course, sturdy, forming corsets which helped to form the ideal figure.

Overcoats were shorter with wider and straighter shoulders. They had straight cuts, widened folds at the back, or had a tight-fitting cut with double or single-breasted buttoning. A redingot cut with long lapels, closed with a single button at the waist, was popular, as was an overcoat without collar with extended upper sections that reached to the neck, with single-breasted buttoning and widened skirt.

Costumes were made with classical cuts. Winter costumes were closed up high, and often featured stand-up collars adorned with fur applications on their entire surface. Short skirts were narrow or widened with inset sections, folding, or pleating, and in 1939 widened into the shape of a bell. French costumes often featured tails that protruded in a bell-shape. In addition to skirts, trousers of straight cut were designed to complement summer costumes of sporty character.

Woolen clothing emphasized the feminine silhouette: they were moderately shortened, were usually undivided at the waist, and featured folding at the neckline, below the breasts, or in vertical seams.

Expected savings in the area of fashionable clothing were announced by designs published in *Eva* magazine and described as "practical, all-purpose clothing" or by drawings of the dresses, combining various kinds of fabrics and complemented by a choice of designs for home-sewing.

MĚSTO V ČERVENCOVÉM ŽÁRU

Jednoduché šaty z pracího hedvábí, šantungu nebo pestrého kretonu, mají místo rukávů jen prodloužené průramky, límec je jen vpředu, kapsy prostřižené s patkou, sukni rozšířenou nadvojitě sežehleny, takže stojí jako hrany.

Drobné obrázky:
Kretonové šaty s malým pestrým vzorkem na bílé půdě, límec malý, kulatý, zapínání na perleťové knoflíky od krku až dolů. Pásek jen vzadu, vpředu dvě kapsy, v postranním švu malé rozparky. Šaty bez rukávů, z rovnatého šantungu. Přes ně bolerko s rovným rukávkem. Bílé nebo světle růžové šaty z plátna, mají stojatý límeček, zapnutý na 1 knoflík, a sedlo s ručně šitými sámečky, 3krát vedle sebe do vzoru barevně vyšitým sedlem.

Retné plátěné šaty s barevně vyšitým sedlem.

Dívčí...
nadrž...
je šír...
našité...
vzadu...

IV

PARISIANA
COMTESSE D'HUMIÈRES

V barevných šatech
do barevné přírody

"City in July heat".
Drawing by Zd. Fuchsová.
Eva, June 15th, 1937

Letní klopený klobouk z anglického vyšívání, zdobený černou sametkou. Model Agnès, foto d'Ora, Paříž.

...pevného veluru,... Bohatý šálový... pod pasem zvo... zdůrazňující "zvonové fasení zadního dílu pláště. Rukavice jsou ušity z téže látky jako plášť (na hřbetu látka, ve dlani kůže).

Plášť z jemného veluru s hořejší částí ze žluté látky, dolejší z látky černé, téže kvality. Zvony na dolejší části jdou kolem dokola. Persiánový límec.

Velurový plášť zelené barvy, jednostranně střižený. Široké vázanky jsou dole zatíženy plotinovou lištou, která je letos velmi módní.

Plášť v barvě korintské červeně se dvěma širokými dutými záhyby.

Coat with bell-shaped tail, drawing by
H. Vlková, Eva, September 15th, 1939

Summer dress, designs by
A. Zenkerová, drawing by
V. Michal, Eva, May 15th, 1938

Tendence: Odstíny barev jsou stále jemnější a každá barva se blíží odstínem barvě sousední. – Favorisované barvy temně červená a lahvově zelená. – Ale viděla jsem i onu krásnou fuchsiově růžovou na šatech ze šifonu a matného sametu. – Na šaty a pláště je hodně temná barva starorůžová, často kombinovaná s hnědou, lahvově zelenou i černou. – Schiaparelli přináší kolekci černou. – Všimla jsem si pláště z velbloudí srsti v barvě chrpově modré. – Tyrkysově modré na příklad v taftu jsou halenky, někdy večerní šaty a doplňky k černým kompletům. – Je mnoho barevných kombinací – na příklad růžová a šedomodrá skládá večerní šaty. Temně červená se kombinuje s temnou šedomodrou. – Do kostymu se nosí bluza z různobarevných sametek.

Paříž v barvách

Volný raglán z anglického tweedu s velkou kostkou. Všimněte si: je bez límce. – Charakteristický plášť podzimní sezony, který přiléhá těsně k tělu, je bez pasu. Na bocích náznak pásu, vliv módy 1900. – Módní tvar: Kolově střižený plášť s hlavním zvonem vzadu. – Charakteristická výzdoba těsného kostymu: persiánové lemy a dlouhé kolmé záševky v pase. Sukně jiné barvy. – Kostym ze tří částí: krátké volné paleto, pod ním kostymový kabátek, u něhož jenom přednice je z materiálu paleta. Záda jsou stejná s materiálem a barvou sukně. – Typický klobouk k odpolednímu kompletu, složený z dvou barev sametu. Záda mód. pláště, rozšířená vloženými záhyby. – Kostíčkový kostymový kabátek pro časný podzim, doplňuje se hladkou sukní.

KRESLILA Z. M. F.

Přížských poznámek HEDY VLKOVÉ,
malířky a majitelky dámského salonu.

Winter costume of black woolen fabric, decorated with black persian, the Hana Podolská fashion house, around 1937, M. D. A., inv.no. 93.253

eva
25

Mail-order patterns were thus far limited to other fashion magazines, such as *Vkus* and *Lada*. The fashion for boleros, which complemented dresses with different materials, provided an opportunity to re-sew older garments. Even formal wear came under attack from short skirts. For less formal occasions from 6:00 p.m. to midnight, evening wear with short skirts was worn. More formal evening toilettes remained long and, thanks to the concentration of fabric at the back, resembled bustle dresses the 1880s. Outfits for young girls were made of organdie or other airy, but durable materials in order to create a new silhouette with tight-fitting bodice and elaborate skirt widened from the hips down. The most practical design for evening wear which came into fashion was a long and wide skirt of black or dark blue tafetta, complemented by a blouse made of lace or either white or pastel organdie.

E. U.

Evening outfit, drawing by Z. Fuchsová, Eva, October 15th, 1939

< Dress with boleros, drawing by M. Kuklová, Eva, April 15th, 1938

Evening outfit for young girls, drawing by H. Vlková, Eva, January 15th, 193

Bílé šifonové šaty mladistvého střihu. Živůtek je celý ručně vysámkován, sukně zvonově střižená do čtyř půlkruhů, aby se docílilo bohatosti, které materiál vyžaduje. V pase šedomodrá grosgrénová stuha.

Šedomodré krepsaténové šaty s hlubokým výstřihem vpředu. Záda jsou zakryta dvěma zvlášť střiženými díly, které končí v kimonovém rukávku. Sukně má napřed šev, aby byla bohatší, a vybíhá do přiléhavého živůtku, uvolněného pouze na prsou náběrami.

Tomatově červené šaty z krepovaného žoržetu, mají sukni řasenou podélně a dlouhý, přepásaný živůtek, řasený příčně.

Černé sametové šaty s měkce rozšířenou sukní. Dva široké pruhy přehozené od zad k ramenům tvoří tu svým ohybem trojúhelník, pod nímž je zapnuta briliantová spona.

Mladistvé bílé šaty z tylově vzdušných krajek. Zvonová sukně se skládá ze tří půlkruhů, z nichž přední je nasazen na jemně nabrané postranní díly. Přes boky je sukně skoro přesně přiléhavá. Dekorativním doplňkem je přehoz, střižený do kulata a ukončený rovnými díly. Jako ozdoba se hodí k šatům briliantový náhrdelník.

KRESLILA H. VLKOVÁ

VYDAVATEL MELANTRICH. PI

"Practical dress
for various pur-
poses", Eva,
April 15th,
1939

Men's Fashion

Economic prosperity, a developing social life, and the ambition of the generation of young Czechoslovaks to draw abreast with Western European nations also influenced men's fashion of the 1920's and 1930's. As elsewhere in the world, men's clothing was characterized by a unity of types and, in consequence, a certain democracy of style. The president and average citizens wore clothing of the same cut. However, exceptional attention was given to the quality of materials used and perfection of tailoring.

The work of the tailor was considered to be a craft, bordering on an art, and was compared to the work of an architect. Based on the knowledge of the human body and the movement of the muscles, the tailor had to create an outfit that fit a real figure and corrected its insufficiencies. Furthermore, the outfit had to allow free movement and fullfil aesthetic requirements.

The cut and material of outfits had to be perfect. Nevertheless, in quality of material as in style, the suit could not appear too flashy, so as not to create the impression that the owner paid too much attention to his dress. A model was the casual elegance of the Prince of Wales, the successor to the English throne. His modern, unconventional, and at the same time extremely elegant manner of dress became a model for men the world over. In Czechoslovakia, the universally recognized authority of Tomáš Garrigue Masaryk of course reached to apparel. He impressed by the classical perfection of formal wear but typical for Masaryk's free-thinking spirit was the riding outfit with military blouse in which on October 28, 1933 the 83 year old gentleman reviewed on horseback a military parade.

While women's dress was predominantly inspired by French fashion, men's fashion was considerably oriented towards England. Men's tailors called themselves "English tailors", and the names of men's fashion houses often featured the word Gentleman. Not only

Evening formal outfit, Pražská moda, autumn–winter 1923/24

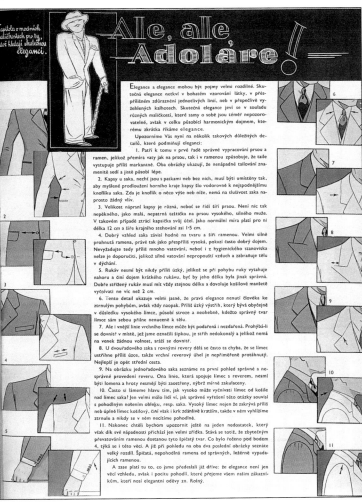

Mistakes in perfect execution of men's jacket, Magazin Rolný, September 1935

OFICIELNÍ ÚBOR: ŽAKET A REDINGOT.

V cizině, na př. v Anglii nebo Francii muž, který nemá ve své kvadrobě žaketu, nemá patrně ani fraku ani smokingu a nechodí nikam, leda na návštěvu k sousedům. Tím chci říci, že Angličan, který není samotář, považuje žaket za toiletní kus naprosto nepostradatelný. Ostatně všude na Derby nebo Grand Prix uvidíte obligátní typ mužů v žaketovém obleku a cylindru.

U nás je tento kabát diskreditován. Nelze se však bez něho obejíti při úřední návštěvě, při recepcích a při vyřizování diplomatických záležitostí, pokud se nekonají večer.

Žaket pracuje se zpravidla z látek shatelandových (Himalaja) barvy černošedé. Je dosti dlouhý a otevřený, šosy sahají až ke kolenům; zapíná se na jeden knoflík. Vesta z téže látky s límečkem. Kalhota k tomuto obleku šije se buď z česané příze nebo z jemného cheviotu, rovně a dole bez záložek. Co se týče obuvi, je třeba lakové botky nebo polobotky rozhodně v kamaši. Bez kamaše byl byste vlastně jen poloobléčen. Rukavice z jelení kůže různých barev nosí se na ruku a řádně zapiaty. Konečně ještě rovný límeček se špičkami, tmavou kravatu široce uvázanou, případně plastron a cylindr nebo tvrdý klobouk, a nevyniknáte-li ničím jiným, tož se nalézáte alespoň v bezvadném obleku žaketovém.

Redingot je obřadní kabát pro starší pány, kteří [...] li o serios[...] přirozeně přijímáni,

chodí na dostihy, na svatby svých synů neb dc[...] kam všude, a tehdy redingot je pro ně podmír[...] úspěchu. Radím, aby si ho dali ušíti z jemného[...] Může být černý nebo šedý, podle okolnosti[...] rovněž z česané příze, poněkud světlejší. Ovšem[...] kabátu kalhoty téže barvy. Ostatní toaletu l[...] stejně ja[...] ku žake[...] daže k[...] nutno v[...] cylindr[...] čistě bíl[...]

NA C[...]

Nechci[...] poručova[...] jel do pro[...] jakých l[...] návštěva[...] u nás s[...] částí dob[...] ať již to[...] Monte[...] Italie.

Jedete[...] cesty, a[...] Biarritz[...] Slovensk[...] poznám[...] nápadno[...] rou se v[...] na nádra[...] nebo u[...] umítece[...] budete[...] čen v tma[...] který v[...] tak pěkn[...] brž v něj[...] dém ne[...] sakovém[...] homespu[...] glického[...] nebo vůbec z hrubé skotské látky, volně střižené[...] šedé kamaše anebo hnědé poloboty s dvojitými po[...] a silné vlněné ponožky. Místo čehokoliv jiného[...] si na hlavu šedou anglickou čepici, na ruce n[...] jelenice patrně také šedé a k dovršení úplnosti ve[...] krčník přibližné barvy, naprosto ne křiklavý.

Všechny šperky zanecháte jistě doma, do m[...] dáte své brillantové knoflíky, je to nejen na ce[...] vkusné, ale trochu i nebezpečné. Přitahujete je[...] podezřelé poutníky.

6

Outfit for walking,
Pražská moda,
autumn—winter
1923/24

Cutaway outfit for
a promenade,
Pražská moda,
autumn—winter
1923/24

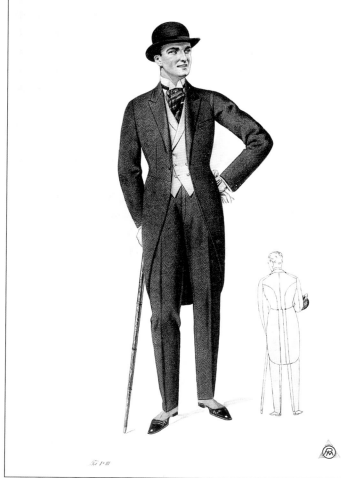

Formal outfit,
Pražská moda,
autumn—winter
1928/29

ČÍSLO 5.   ZIMA 1935/36.   ROČNÍK XXXVIII.

AKADEMICKÉ MÓDNÍ LISTY

Odborný časopis, věnovaný módě a umění stříhačskému.
Orgán „První módní akademie krejčovské" v Praze.
Hlavní spolupracovníci v Paříži, Londýně a v Praze.

Odpovědný redaktor Jan Kratina, jun.

Sešit 5.   **Cena Kč 5.-**

Redakce i administrace
Praha I.-463,
Melantrichova ul. 15.
Telefon 336-24.

Vydavatel a nakladatel
JAN KRATINA,
majitel „První akademie krejčovské
v Praze I.-463, Melantrichova 15.

Gentleman

TRENCH-COAT

Doba, kdy v deštivém a nejistém počasí sahalo se k nejstarším zásobám šatstva, kterým se říkalo „šaty do deště", již minula. I u nás vítězí už praktický a při tom elegantní vkus Angličana i oblékáme do chladného, sychravého neb deštivého počasí „Trench-coat". Tento moderní, praktický a decentní kus oděvu splňuje veškeré požadavky, které jsou naň kladeny. Jest trvanlivý, protože zhotoven z výborných, pevných a nezničitelných látek, jež lze mýti třeba „rýžákem", dále jest naprosto nepromokavý a to nejen kvalitou vrchní látky, nýbrž hlavně vložkami, z nichž vložka z jemného impregnovaného plátna odolá i nejsilnějšímu náporu vlhka. V teplém počasí nosí se „trench-coat" bez teplé vložky, v zimě s odepínací vložkou z velbloudí srsti.

Různými střihy trench-coatů pánských i dámských vyhovuje se účelu jejich hlavního použití: buď pro sport a namáhavé tury, nebo pro město. Městské trench-coaty jsou kromě obvyklé šedavé barvy šity též z modré látky. V nejnovější době podařilo se firmě: *Bratří Šulcové, Praha I.*, Kaprová 13 získati pro RČS zastoupení známých anglických, prvotřídních trench-coatů značky: *"The Stormgard"* za velmi přístupné ceny, takže bude tím umožněno zavésti tento praktický způsob oblékání i u nás. Pláště "The Stormgard" vyrábějí se ve třech druzích sportovních střihů, dále pláště městské ve dvou druzích a trench-coaty dámské.

WIND CUFFS
TEDDY FLEECE
SUPER GRADE GABARDINE
STORMPROOF GABARDINE LINING
STORMGARD OILSKIN INTERLINING

Fantastická móda

V poslední době je z Francie propagována móda, která znamená návrat k časům krále Ludvíka XIV., totiž ony krátké kalhotky ke kolenům, které se mají nositi ať již ke fraku nebo sportovnímu oděvu. Mnozí nazvali tuto módu fantastickou. Móda se však fantastice vymyká. Co bylo za krále Ludvíka a mělo by býti ještě dnes, nemá v sobě přece fantasie, tak jako kdyby přicházely do módy sutany, železná brnění, tógy nebo sametové kabátce. Teprve něco, co ještě tu nebylo, mělo by jakýsi nárok na fantastický přívlastek, ovšem v té věci bude rozhodovat nejen tvar, nýbrž i materiál oděvu. Za příklad skvěle slouží třináctá kapitola románu „Zavražděný básník".*)

_____

*) Nákl. „Aventina".

Podzimní plášť do deště ze světle
hnědého gabardinu. Praktický
rain-coat ze světlého cordu,
vhodný pro podzimní chladné
dny. — Raglán pro zimu z šedé
diagonál silné anglické látky.
Hodí se na ulici, na cesty, do auta.

beneath the bottom of the coat. Only a narrow strip of waistcoat was revealed during movement. A smooth white shirt was fitted with a firm shirt-front. It was recommended that the shirt be buttoned in the entire length of the front so that it would not have to be put on over the head. The collar was low with downturned points, complemented by a bow tie of white batiste or piqué. The elegance was finished off with details: cuff-links of pearls or mother-of-pearl, the same as the single button on the shirt-front, a casually tied bow tie, long black silk or yarn socks, patent leather shoes, and a matt tophat.

The return of the formal evening suit with tails in no case signified a decline in popularity of the dinner suit. In the mid 1920s, the dinner suit ("smoking") had a slightly tight-fitting cut which had to be comfortable enough so that it would not hinder free movement, especially during dancing. The dinner jacket was closed with one button at the waist. Its front parts were rounded and the wide lapels were covered with matt silk.

∧ Men's fashion in autumn
and winter 1933, Eva,
October 15th, 1933 >

the elegant form of evening dress and casual and comfortable sporty style of day wear, but also individual kinds of outfits together with their English names were adopted from English fashion.

A strict etiquette of dress held sway through the entire inter-war period which demanded a special kind of clothing for every occasion and time of day. After the chaos of the First World War, evening dress once became the appropriate outfit for more formal social occasions. It was restrained, but thought through to the last detail in order to attain a slender, elegant silhouette that only slightly indicated the contours of the figure. The shoulders were straight, the front parts were formed with breast darts and reached to slightly below the hips, while in the back swallow-shaped tails extended to the knees. The matching suit pants were long, wide, and fitted with a silk band inserted in the side seam of each leg. As part of the suit was a white, single-breasted waistcoat with collar that was closed with three buttons. The bottom of the waistcoat ended in obtuse points which were not supposed to extend

...................Trenchcoat, Gentleman, 1927, no. 7

Svrchník z tmavomodrého neb
šedomodrého ratiné, nejnovější
střih pro letošní zimu. — Kost-
kovaný plášť ze silné anglické
látky s velkými našívanými kapsami a odepínací koženou podšívkou. — Tweedový nebo ho-
mespunový sportovní oblek pro
podzimní sporty.

PACHNER

KRESLIL V. PACHNER

Převládající jarní linie

ve všech svrchních oděvech je v letošní jarní módě, jak již zde bylo správně předpovězeno, volná. Móda se vrací plně k formě anglické, která je nám daleko přístupnější, než francouzská móda, v pasu zúžená. A i Paříž přiklonila se letos ke splývající široké formě svrchních oděvů. Je to pochopitelné, poněvadž volná linie je jednoduchá a vše jednoduché lahodí oku.

Je to sice po tailované módě, která vládla nyní po několik sezon, dosti nezvyklé a každému se zdá, že v takovém moderním plášti vypadá příliš široký. Není ale tomu tak. Volný angl. střih vyrovnává, abych tak řekl, plně rozdíly mezi štíhlými a silnými postavami, t. j. činí štíhlou postavu ramenatější a širší, aniž by bylo zapotřebí přehnaného vyplňování ramen vatou, které je přece jen

umělé a vypadá v důsledku toho nepřirozeně, obzvláště když přecházelo z vycpaných ramen do úzkého pasu. U postav silných zase vyrovnává splývající forma vystupování pasové linie a tím že kabát tohoto moderního střihu tvoří od ramenou dolů jednu rovnou linii, činí prsa širší a i hodně silnou postavu štíhlejší.

Především vidíte na obr. 1 látkový raglán, uzavřený až ke krku, s kimonorukávy, jenž čím je volnější, tím lépe vypadá. Tvoří od ramena až dolů jak vpředu, tak i vzadu volnou, svislou linii. Takovéto kabáty mohou býti zhotoveny z homespunu, gabardinu, covercoatu nebo dokonce i ve vzorku rybí páteře. Je praktický, poněvadž právě tak dobře sluší v plném jarním slunci, jako je užitečný v dešti.

Sportovní oblek (obr. 2) liší se poněkud od loňského střihu. Sako má delší revér, je méně zúžené v pasu a dostalo tím také volnější formy, ačkoliv tailování je posud znatelné, ale pouze nepatrně. Golfky, sahající do půl lýtka, doplňují tento líbivý a praktický sportovní a výletní oděv. Je z látky anglických vzorů nebo sportexu, po případě i fresca. Nosí se k takovému obleku anglická čepice, sportovní jednobarevná košile s přišitým límcem a pestrá vázanka, po případě i pullover.

Na obr. 3 vidíme jarní raglán volného střihu, dvouřadový na 4 knoflíky,

širší revers a zakulacení předních krajů nepočíná již od prostředního knoflíku, nýbrž až od spodního, čímž je linie kraje více lomená ve střední části a více zakulacená ve svém přechodu do vodorovné. Také v pasu není sako již tak silně probráno jako dříve. Kalhoty se nenosí již tak široké, jak kdysi byly v oblibě.

Jarní letošní móda skýtá v každém směru, jak v látkách, tak i tvarech, tolik rozmanitostí, že v ní každý nalezne to, co mu nejlépe sluší. Látky se neváží na určitý vzorek, nosí se pro obleky vzorky s páskem, hladké jednobarevné látky, pepř a sůl, ba i karo se objevuje. Co se týče barev, zůstává stále ještě oblíbena šedá pro svou praktičnost, ale také se hojněji objevují barvy zelená, hnědá a modrá. Význačnou vlastností módy je pásek jinobarevný, v šedé půdě modrý, zelený, hnědý a červený a obdobně i v ostatních barvách. Velikou módou je vzorek, zvaný ,,tennis'', to jest jednobarevná látka s řidšími jednoduchými pásky.

Je tedy volnosti ve výběru víc než dost a tím vlastně móda přestává býti předpisem, nýbrž úplně se podřizuje osobnímu vkusu.

V. Wobořil.

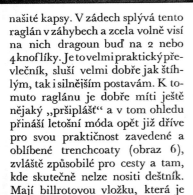

našité kapsy. V zádech splývá tento raglán v záhybech a zcela volně visí na nich dragoun buď na 2 nebo 4 knoflíky. Je to velmi praktický převlečník, sluší velmi dobře jak štíhlým, tak i silnějším postavám. K tomuto raglánu je dobře míti ještě nějaký ,,pršiplášť'' a v tom ohledu přináší letošní móda opět již dříve pro svou praktičnost zavedené a oblíbené trenchcoaty (obraz 6), zvláště způsobilé pro cesty a tam, kde skutečně nelze nositi deštník. Mají billrotovou vložku, která je

činí absolutně nepromokavými i v největších lijácích, musí býti robustně stavěny a proto jsou poněkud těžší. Hodí se pro svou absolutní nepromokavost také výborně pro vojsko, finanční stráž, četnictvo a každého, kdo po celé hodiny musí nepřetržitě býti v každém lijáku v přírodě. Pro vysloveně sportovní účely se hodí nejlépe covercoatový plášť, potažený svrchu černou gumovou vrstvou (obr. 4). Je taktéž spolehlivě nepromokavý a tím se stává svrchním oděvem, hodícím se výborně·pro motocykl, lov a do přírody vůbec. Pro město jsou nadále v oblibě pláště z gumovaného balonového plátna, balonového hedvábí a režného plátna, které se dělají ve střihu obr. 1. Jsou laciné, lehké a skýtají také spolehlivou ochranu proti dešti.

Jarní oblek (obr. 5) má oproti dřívějším střihům jen nepatrné úchylky. Sako má

Winter coat, Pražská
moda, autumn–winter
1923/24

The suit pants had the same cut as those of the evening suit with tails, but without the silk band running down the legs. The waistcoat of the dinner suit was without collar, sewn from the same material as the coat, and was closed with four buttons. The matching shirt had a low collar with long downturned points and a shirtfront. Shirtfronts for dancing were starched, while for other occasions they were soft. In 1924, *Gentleman* magazine claimed that young Americans were trying to introduce turned collars with their dinner suits. The bow tie worn with the dinner suit was supposed to be black and quite wide. In the second half of the 1920s a double-breasted dinner suit gained in popularity which was considered to be less official evening wear than the single-breasted dinner suit. A shirt with soft shirt-front was worn with it that was so tightly closed that the waistcoat was unnecessary. After 1925 a fashionable colour for formal evening wear was a very deep marine blue called "the midnight blue".

It was possible to somewhat relax the formal character of the dinner jacket during summer evenings, when etiquette allowed men to wear a light jacket with white piqué or silk waistcoat, or without waistcoat, complemented by a shirt decorated with folds. For summer dancing, instead of a dinner suit, a gentleman could dress in only a dancing jacket with long lapels, closed with two buttons.

From magazines, Czechoslovak men were well informed about the etiquette of evening dress and fashion currents, although statistics published in *Gentleman* magazine in 1929 prove that Prague men did not care much about either. The writer of the article claimed that in The London Pavilion Theatre in London, 35 % of the men in the audience were dressed in evening coat with tails, 62 % wore single-breasted and 3 % double-breasted dinner suits, while at the evening performance of a "high-society theatre in Prague" the reporter encountered two men in dinner jackets, four in cutaways, and none in evening suits with tails. However, one-third of the male visitors wore suits composed of a dark jacket and striped pants, and two-thirds wore walking outfits.[98]

For official and ceremonial occasions that took place during the day, social etiquette required a cutaway or frock-coat. However, criticism appeared in magazines maintainting that in Czechoslovakia such types of formal social dress was neglected and inappropriately replaced, either with jacket suits or dinner suits. The reason for this lay not only in the high prices of these specific and relatively infrequently used suits, but also in their disrepute, since both cutaway and frock-coat were related to the bureaucratic ritual of the Austro-Hungarian past of the new state. On the other hand a cutaway and top hat were commonly worn by the young men of the Baťa factories in Zlín, selected for leading position and to repre-

Moderní jednořadové sako

s vysokými a širokými rameny, v pase přiléhací, s prsními prostřihy. — Zapíná se dvěma knoflíky. Klopy dolu sestřižené.

Přesné střihy podle tohoto vyobrazení a každé míry obdržíte v »První Akademii krejčovské« v Praze I., Melantrichova ul. čís. 15.

Modern single-breasted jacket, Akademické Módní Listy, spring 1934

sent the firm abroad, as marks of class and good manners. These young men were trained together in a modern home called Tomášov according to the model of the best English boarding houses with an emphasis on sport, the study of foreign languages, and selected social manners.[99] The cutaway was usually made of Shetland fabrics of black-grey colour. It was quite long, open, closed with a single button, and with tails reaching to the knees at the back. The waistcoat was made of the same material. It was straight at the bottom, double-breasted, closed high to the neck, and had a collar. The matching trousers to the cutaway were usually made of different, often striped fabric. They were straight and without cuffs. Comple-menting the cutaway was a shirt with folded collar, a neckpiece in the shape of a plastron, and patent leather shoes, always worn with spats. Even more formal was a frock-coat which was close to the traditional type of "Kaiserrock" with double-breasted coat reaching to the knees, cut at the waist, and somewhat loosefitting with silk lapels and wide turned-down collar. It was made of fine black or grey cheviot. The matching trousers were made of the same material as the coat, and were grey if worn with a grey coat, or, when worn with black, of a somewhat lighter shade. The frock coat was strictly worn with a tophat and pure white spats. The suit was meant to be worn at weddings and horseraces.

For other occasions, a jacket suit was appropriate, sewn either traditionally from one material, or, as was especially popular around 1925, in combination, with two different materials. The suit could consist of a darker jacket and lighter trousers, or a jacket without pattern together with striped or checked trousers. For five o'clock tea, a black jacket with waistcoat of similar colour

The president of Czechoslovakia Dr. Edvard Beneš with Prime Minister Dr. Milan Hodža, Pestrý týden, December 28th, 1935

and light-grey cheviot trousers were appropriate. Such a suit was complemented by a shirt with hard collar and dark tie with minute pattern. The winter season of 1924 — 25 witnessed a change in fashion line which became evident to various extent in all kinds of men's clothing. In contrast to earlier fashion, characterized by the "taille", taken in at the waist, the new line was loose, not tight-fitting, with shorter jacket and trousers reaching only to the shoes. Of course, already in the years 1926 — 27, the waist again became more pronounced and all kinds of jackets were further shortened as far as just below the seat. Details were not prescribed. Both single-breasted jackets, closed with two or three buttons, and double-breasted jackets, closed with two pairs of buttons, were fashionable. The double-breasted type of jacket became especially popular around 1928, when it became a part of social, dancing, walking, and working suits. In the 1920s, even in the greatest heat, on formal occasions it was not permitted to take off the jacket, to unbutton the shirtcollar, shirt, or waistcoat, or even not to wear a waistcoat. A suit without lining was created for the hottest days in the city. It was made of fabrics known in Czechoslovakia as "fresco-tropical". They were light, thin, almost transluscent, and airy.

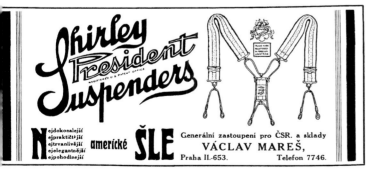

The inner-seams were edged with the same material as the suit. A linen suit was recommended for summer stays in the countryside.

The warmest outer garment for men in the 1920s was a fur coat — ie. a woolen outer layer with fur lining and fur collar. Men's fur coats were of several types. Fur coats for daily wear reached to just above the knees or only somewhat further, usually with a covering of gaberdine of grey, brown, or inconspicuous tones of green or blue colour. The lining could be of bisam, nutria, hamster, while the collar could be made of opossum, otter, silk, persian, or beaver. Fur coats for more formal occasions were longer, with an outer layer of black molton. There were complemented by a tophat and, according to a pithy comment in *Gentleman* magazine, also a car with chauffeur. Fur coats for sports were, in contrast, shorter and incorporated as lining less valuable furs. Fur coats for travelling distinguished themselves by being the longest, sewn from homespun or napped coating, with a lining of lamb's wool or fleece, and a raccoon collar.

The most modern type of winter coat in 1924 was a single-breasted overcoat made of dark, preferably black material, closed with hidden buttons, and with a velvet collar. It had sturdy shoulders and a silhouette with a slightly dilated waistline, an effect created by the manner of ironing rather than the cut of the garment. This overcoat, well-padded and backstitched on the inside, was considered by *Gentleman* magazine to be by far the most elegant coat in comparison with similar padded overcoats with fur collars.

The fur or winter coat of the 1920s was replaced in spring by a raglan. Raglans were worn for taking walks or on journeys, protected the wearer from bad weather, and provided warmth in cold temperatures. Its looseness permitted comfortable and unrestricted movement. It was made of half-thick material, had a loose cut,

Men's outfit for skiing,
the Josef Eiselt company,
Prague 1931, M. D. A.,
inv.no. 97.976

Moderní dvouřadové sako

dvěma knoflíky zapínané, třetí pár ozdobou. Ramena normální šíře, mírně vatovaná. Prsní prostřihy. Rukávy s rozparkem na 3 knoflíčky.

Přesné střihy podle tohoto vyobrazení a každé míry obdržíte v „První Akademii krejčovské" v Praze I., Melantrichova ul. čís. 15.

Modern double-breasted jacket,
Akademické Módní Listy, winter 1935/36

was slightly tight-fitting at the waist, and comfortable in the shoulders. It was double-breasted, closed with three or four pairs of buttons. The collar and lapels were wide. The pockets could be of inset or patch type. In the back there sometimes was a belt. All seams were stitched several times over. Raglan coats did not have to have raglan sleeves. Sewn of light woolen flannel, it was used as a sporty coat over a tennis outfit. The ulster coat was meant for especially uncomfortable weather with rain or snow. It was a big, wide, and long coat of a straight cut, with wide collar and lapels, single- or double-breasted, straight at the back, and without a belt.

Even less warm than the raglan was the topcoat, usually sewn from light brown or light grey covercoat or shetland. It was very loose, closed at the neck with short lapels, with a slit at the back. It was usually single-breasted; nevertheless, a

šlím o jaru, přivolá-
o ně nehnul prstem,
k nakonec vysedí ze
a. Sledujte, pánové,
nati lyrickým před-
tickému rozechvění,
fialek, naslouchejte,
lechněte si i spodní
krve a já nevím, co
dravý rozum, položte
ě, máte-li pro tento
poslyšte.
s myšlenku pohybu,
ený byl ušit z látek
i dobrou jakostí i le-
átky sportovní jsou
en z nejčistší vlny,
oslední známky jsou
i kostkami. (U ame-
tka corduroys, druh
nlivost a odolnost.)
jlepší. Nejde tu ani
eriál. Dokonce příliš
i dělá nutně dojem
tu zachovati dobrý
nulých dobách, kdy
tech. Ve sportovním
rásné harmoničnosti
ěc!), dopřávajíce si
osti. Dojista podle
ěláte, se obléknete.
etu či golfovou hůl,
e přioděn. Dnes už
dress. Kůží podšité
olkové jupky s knik-
rávníkovému". Bílé

Jednoduchost, která je vůbec moderní, měla vliv i na
typ sportovního obleku. Vymohla, že zmizely všeliké
zbytečné titěrnosti, jako: našité záhyby, sedlová záda,
pasy atd. Moderní sportovní kabát vlastně je totéž jako
obyčejné sako. Střih i linie nemají nic speciálního. Arci
takový golfový kabát je něco jiného. V posledních dobách
jevila se snaha po odlišení od sportovní uniformovanosti.
Tak začaly *sportovní obleky kombinované,* které jsme už
znali z modelů úboru jezdeckého: černý kabát a šedé
spodky. Muž, který má svůj vlastní vkus, může po této
stránce samostatně kombinovati. Zásadou bývá: jednobarevné sako anebo se vzorkem, jenž je příbuzný vzorku
na spodkách. Breeches se nenosí. Ale spodky nesmí býti
tmavšího tónu než kabát.

Na hřišti se uplatňuje nyní místo vlněné sportovní vesty,
ještě loni tak velmi oblíbené, nový druh sweatru „*pul-
lower*". Je to anglická věc, typická svým orientálským
barevným vzorkem. Má buď oválný nebo špičatý výstřih, ale bez zapínání. Staří sportsmani zůstávají ovšem
při kamzičích vestách s hedvábnými rukávy.

double-breasted version exists with a quarter
belt at the back. Pockets were inset. All seams
were sewn two or three times over, with the
lower edge sewn five times over.

In the course of the 1920s, numerous other
variations of men's overcoats became popular.
They usually had English names, such as an
overcoat used for visits called "Chesterfield",
made of black or dark grey shetland, and with
a cut similar to that of a winter coat; a double-breasted overcoat called "polo-coat"; or a
double-breasted raglan coat called "guard-
coat". Around 1927 a "trench-coat" appeared
in Czech men's fashion that was recommended for damp and cold weather. It was made
waterproof and warm by a detachable lining
of fine impregnated linen, and a second detachable lining of camel hair. It was single- or
double-breasted with inset or raglan sleeves.
It had wide lapels and collar, and was bound
at the waist by a belt.

In the 1930s, the modern lifestyle and general
popularity of sports created an ideal of a man
with a tall athletic figure, broad shoulders, and
slender waist. This ideal brought with it a
somewhat looser, more comfortable style
of men's clothing, half tight-fitting, with wide,
straight shoulders, and a dilated waist. The
trousers were loose, with several folds at the
waist, and with cuffs at the bottom. As with
women's fashion, in which in the 1930s all garments became longer, in men's clothing longer
jackets and trousers, folded at shoe-level, became popular. The tails of evening suits also
became longer, reaching below the knees.
Overcoats also increased in length.

Sporting clothing, Gentleman, 1925, no. 4

The significant role that sport played in the life of the man of the 1920s and 1930s placed greater demands on sporting wear. The basic demand was for quality material, permitting free movement, comfort, and easy care. Among the best materials were homespun, loden, tweed, cheviot, whipcord, corduroy, as well as jersey and tricot, or new fabrics such as "sportex", "traveltex", and "smartex". Knitted wear became more and more widespread. The sporty style required a comfortable cut, and at the same time it permitted certain unusual features in the cut as well as more decoration, which, however, was not allowed to be too conspicuous. In the 1920s, every kind of sport had its own individual kind of dress. The outfits differed in their jackets, while trousers were the same for most sports. The trousers worn were usually knickers. Around 1925 such trousers were not wide-spread in Czechoslovakia, but they were increasingly recommended for their comfort and practicality. They had to be perfectly sewn — long and wide enough in order to flow loosely over the knees, where they were gathered up by a strap. They were usually worn with woolen patterned, most often checked, knee-highs, or with long linen leggings for mountaineering.

For golf, the knickers were complemented by a "Norfolk" jacket, with patch pockets, often with a yoke, and with a back decorated with folds, pulled together by a belt at the back. For walks or automobile trips, knickers were worn with a comfortable flannel jacket, further complemented by a leather or waterproof overcoat, or comfortable woolen ulster for car rides. Leather pants and a leather jacket were worn for riding on a motorcycle. At the end of the 1920s, the leather jacket was hitched up at the waist and closed with a zipper. For motorcycle riding one could also wear overalls, which could also be worn as work clothes.

Around 1925, tennis outfits became more colourful: the pure whiteness of trousers and open shirt gained an alternative with grey flannel trousers, white jackets with coloured stripes, and colourfully edged white waistcoats with long sleeves.

Sport clothes also included single-coloured or patterned silk and flannel shirts with patch pockets, complemented by colour ties of foulard, raw silk, or knitwear.

A favorite part of all kinds of sporty outfits was a knitted sweater, which could have the form of a waistcoat with long sleeves, closed at the front, or the form of a turtleneck. A new kind of garment was the pullover, a sweater of English origin with v-neck, either with long sleeves or sleeveless. The head could be covered with a flat sporty cap of an English type with visor, or with a soft felt hat. The contemporary sportsman wore shoes of thick leather with a double outsole or, as a new hit, shoes with rubber soles.

Skiing sports were still dominated by Norwegian dress, consisting of loose, belted coats reaching to below the hips, fitted with patch pockets, and long, wide trousers bound with a strap at the ankles. At the same time, a hood of waterproof material was recommended. Its variation was an anorak with ties at the sides and at the neck.

In the 1920s, officially required swim wear was a tricot with athletic shirt, complemented by a terry-fabric bathing robe. However, numerous photographs of Czech outdoor swimming pools and ponds show that men chose comfort over etiquette, preferring swimming shorts. Nevertheless, it was necessary to observe formal rules for sailing: a dark blue jacket with gold buttons had to be complemented by white flannel trousers, white shoes, and a flat white cap. For canoeing, shorts and tricot athletic shirt sufficed.

E. U.

< L. Richter – A. Jonáš: Even a stone melts for the fur from the Junger company, Moravská Ostrava, printed by Melantrich Praha, around 1935

PRODEJNY:

ČEKAN.
Václavské nám. Jungmanova ul.

KLOBOUK

SICHROVSKÝ.
Celetná 32

WEISS. Celetná 42

STYL

řečí. Neboť jest rozdíl mezi přednáškou a řečí. A založil si rodinný život.

Když bylo jeho synkovi asi deset let, zavedl ho na místa svého mládí a řekl: „Házej dřívka do vody a zamýšlej se nad prcháním života. Pozoruj hřbety pracujících a mysli na radosti života. Zahleď se do koruny kopretiny a všimni si, jak se točí za sluncem. Pozoruj vandráka a pozoruj jásavé reklamy velkoměsta. Naplňuj svou duši smutkem, ideály, moudrostí a zkušeností. A pak ve vhodném okamžiku promluv. Raději dříve než později. Tehdy se i za tebou budou točit kopretiny."

*

Muž, jenž krotce trpí, aby nad něho předčili lidé, kteří k tomu nemají práva, a jenž nemá snahy ani touhy povznésti se nad jiné, je jistě nízkého ducha. Tato slabost vyplývá obyčejně z netečnosti nebo z dobromyslnosti, jakož i z nechuti k všelikému hluku a shonu. Ale tato slabost bývá vždy provázena litováním ...
Ad. Smith.

*

ZAJÍMAVÝ AMERICKÝ PÁNSKÝ MÓDNÍ ČASOPIS

přinášející na 200 stranách krásného papíru nesčetná vyobrazení z americké a anglické společnosti a ukázky posledních druhů prádla, kravat, klobouků, obuvi, swetrů a pulloverů, rovněž i sportovních úborů a potřeb, poslední pánské obleky a jiné — vyskytl se tyto dny i v Praze a bude jistě nepostradatelnou pomůckou všem oborům pánskou módou se zabývajícím. Je to „MEN'S WEAR". Další viz insert.

Stoleté jubileum límečku

Zvláštní stoleté jubileum slaví nyní Amerika, totiž jubileum vynalezení pánského límečku. Vynalezla jej Američanka náhodou. Jako při tak mnohých vynálezech, tak i zde byla vůdčí myšlenkou snaha zjednodušiti si práci. Až do té doby byl límeček nerozlučně spojen s kosilí, a byl-li pošpiněný, musela se práti i celá košile. Jistý americký obuvník, jménem Montagu, žijící ve Troy ve státě New Yorku, držel velmi na čistotu svého oděvu a nechtěl nositi košile, jejichž límeček byl jen poněkud pošpiněn. Jeho žena byla proto velmi přetížena stálým praním, a když jí jednoho dne zas vracel košili posud čistou s límečkem pošpiněným, utrhla jej ve zlosti od košile. Když pak zlostná a přece zarmoucená hotovila se přišíti límeček, napadla jí geniální myšlenka: proč nevynechati límeček oddělený od košile, proč nevyprati jej zvlášť a nepřipevniti knoflíčky k čisté košili? Kolik práce si ušetří, učiní-li tak se všemi košilemi mužovými? Řečeno, provedeno! Byla to ona, která darovala límci po prvé jeho „vlastní život", a její opatření prokázalo se být tak praktickým, že její příklad následovaly všechny její sousedky. Tak povstal moderní pánský límec, který se od té doby stal tak důležitou součástkou mužského oděvu.
N. P.

Notes

Gentleman 1925, č. 8

1) Pětiletí Ženské národní rady. Ženská rada IV,
1928, no. 8, p. 130.

2) Plamínková, F. F.: Několik poznámek o práci
čsl. žen. Ženská rada V, 1929, no. 2, p. 18.

3) Ženští poslanci a senátoři po volbách 27.10.1929.
Ženská rada V, 1929, no. 9, p. 124.

4) Ullrich, Z.: Několik čísel o středoškolském a vysoko-
školském studiu žen. Eva XI, 1939, no. 3, p. 14.

5) Vostřebalová, V: Deset let organizace sociální práce
po r. 1918. Ženská rada VIII, 1932, p. 86.

6) Uspěchy ženské práce. Ženská rada IV, 1928,
no. 8, p. 133.

7) Smržová, A: Kam po maturitě. Eva VIII, 1936,
no. 15, p. 7.

8) Závodová, J. H.: Žena ministerským radou.
Eva X, 1938, p. 9.

9) Závodová, J. H.: VIII. výroční sjezd ústředí čs.
hospodyň. Eva X, 1938, no. 13, p. 27.

10) Mayer, J.: Reforma manželského práva. Eva VIII,
1936, no. 10, p. 26.

11) Plamínková, F. F.: Zpráva o činnosti Výboru pro
volební právo žen Mezinárodní Alliance v Berlíně
v červnu 1929. Ženská rada V, 1929, no. 6, p. 77.

12) Pujmanová, M.: Dnešní žena. Eva VII, 1934,
no. I, p. 31.

13) Opalujeme se. Měsíc, 1932, no. 8, pp. 32-33.

14) Schieszlová, O.: Mladá žena československá.
Eva X, 1938, no. 10, p. 12.

15) Smržová, A.: A zase pensionáty, věno a honba
za manželem? Eva VIII, 1935, no. 3, p. 25.

16) Co vykonala ČNR v těchto dnech. Ženská
rada XIV, 1938, p. 147.

17) Eva X, 1938, no. 21, p. 5.

18) The magazine "Wiener Mode" appeared in 1893 in
Czech translation under the title "Nové Mody". Besides
this, "Pařížské Mody" appeared in Prague between 1893
and 1894. In 1895 both publications were united under
the name "Nové Pařížské Mody" as the Czech version
of the magazine "Wiener Mode".

19) Gentleman I, 1924, no. I, p. 4.

20) Paříž v Praze. Modní revue VII, 1927, no. 43, p. 4.

21) Uchalová, E.: Od valčíku po tango II. Česká
móda 1870-1914, Praha 1994, p. 29.

22) Chytilův Adresář hl. m. Prahy 1924-25, p. 492, 481,
589 etc.

23) Kraus, O.: Vznik, snahy a účel "Pražské Mody".
Pražská Moda I, no. I, Autumn-Winter 1923-24, p. I.

24) Lysková, E.: Textilní tvorba. In: Výtvarná
kultura v Brně 1918-1938, Brno 1993, pp. 70-72

25) Adresář král. hl. m. Prahy a obcí sousedních.
Praha 1910. Vol. II, p. 172

26) Chytilův Adresář hl. m. Prahy, 1924-25, p. 510.

27) Elegantní Praha II, 1923, no. 3, p. 12.

28) Elegantní Praha III, 1925, no. 2, p. 28.

29) E. Rosenbaumová is noted here as a producer of ready-made clothing and a tailor; Adresář král. hl. m. Prahy a obcí sousedních. Praha 1910. Vol. II, pp. 141, 172.

30) See note 26.

31) Lamarová, M., Kybalová, L.: Oděvní tvorba. Praha 1986, p. 6.

32) Niko Pauzdr mentioned this in conversations with PhDr. Helena Jarošová.

33) Lamarová, M., Kybalová, L.: l. c., p. 14. Kybalová, L.: Fuchsová Zdeňka. In: Nová encyklopedie českého výtvarného umění, Prague 1996, Volume I, p. 192.

34) Mandlová, A.: Dneska už se tomu směju. Praha 1990, pp. 42-43.

35) According to the recollections of Zdeňka Fuchsová-Mayerová, preserved in her family, after the show had finished she rode by taxi through Paris and made the first drawings in her sketch book. A number of these are part of her estate and are in the possession of the Museum of Decorative Arts in Prague.

36) Recollections of Růžena Kautská, seamstress at the Rosenbaum fashion house.

37) Information from the family of Zdeňka Fuchsová-Mayerová. In Paris Fuchsová supposedly also visited Mrs. Simpsonová on business.

38) Podolský, V.: Královna naší módy. Večerní Praha 11. 10. 1991.

39) Lamarová, M., Kybalová, L.: l. c., p. 10. Jarošová, H.: Vlková Hedvika. In.: Nová encyklopedie českého výtvarného umění, Prague 1996, Volume II., p. 910. Rousová, H.: Vobecký František, l. c., p. 911.

40) Elegantní Praha I, 1922, no. 1-2, p. 18.

41) Elegantní Praha I, 1922, no. 3-4, p. 32.

42) Elegantní Praha I, 1922, no. 7-8, p. 54.

43) Elegantní Praha I, 1922, no. 9-10, p. 61. Elegantní Praha II, 1923-24, no. 4, p. 53.

44) Elegantní Praha II, 1923-24, no. 7, unpaginated.

45) Elegantní Praha I, 1922, no. 7-8, p. 51.

46) Elegantní Praha II, 1923-24, no. 4, p. 58.

47) Elegantní Praha II, 1923-24, no. 3, pp. 11-12.

48) Modní revue VII, 1927, no. 42, p. 7..

49) Měsíc III, 1934, no. 7, p. 7.

50) Modní revue VII, 1927, no. 16, p. 11.

51) Rolný, A.: Z dějin podniku Rolný. Rolný magazin 1935, no. 3.

52) Naše služba I, Prostějov 1933, p. 1.

53) Elegantní Praha II, 1923-24, no. 3, p. 12.

54) Francoise Tétart-Vittu wrote on these issues in detail in the newspaper articles: "Petite introduction pour un sujet multiple" and "Des Menues Plaisir au Studio de Couture, in Le Dessin sous toutes les coutures, catalog to the exhibition of the same name in the Palais Galliera, Musée de la Mode et du Costume, which took place in Paris April 27-August 13, 1995.

55) Given the normal tasks of fashion artists, drawing decorations and ornaments was not so very different. Vlková recalled that beginning when she first started working for the Podolská fashion house, she mainly drew monograms on the clothes of customers, motifs for embroidery and other details. Francoise Tétart-Vittu in the earlier cited catalog also notes a certain correlation between people who attended courses in ornamental drawing and later designers (modeliste) and draughtswomen.

56) The author of this article relies to a great deal on conversations which she conducted during the first half of the 1980s with Hedvika Vlková regarding the beginnings of her professional work and the general situation of Czech fashion from the 1910s through the 1960s.

57) This fact was noted by Xavier Chaumette in the article "La Figurine de mode: histoire d'une pédagogie", published in the already cited catalog on page 41, 44.

58) Packer, W.: Dessins de mode. Vogue, 1923-83, Herscher, Paris 1989, p. 8.

59) Packer, W.: l. c., p. 104. Vogue, September 1963, USA, pp. 184-189. Art Fashion, Zurich 1992.

60) Compare for example the magazine MO-NO (Modní novinky) and album Morava, Brno 1947, library of the Museum of Decorative Arts in Prague.

61) The name Rigo Schönborn figures in "Elegantní Praha" as the creator of illustrated covers. We are informed that "before the war he worked for the leading Parisian magazines."

62) The author took this information from H. Vlková and Niko Pauzdr. In "Kniha o reklamě" (The Book about Advertising) /Reklamní klub v Praze, Praha 1940/ we find on page 408: "School of Advertising and Fashion Drawing, formerly Rotter, now of arch. Jedlička, Prague II, Vodičkova street 32". Here see also the supplement on page 224.

63) See the conversations which the author of the article conducted with Hedvika Vlková.

64) In the first issues of "Pražská moda" as well as for example "Drobné umění" from 1924 we also find appeals to "all painters and to Czech art" which state that the association Pražská moda is looking for a Czech painter and artist who would like to work on designs for men's and women's lines of fashion and who would be "...very well paid".

65) In the catalogue to "Český funkcionalismus 1920-1940" (UPM v Praze a Moravská galerie v Brně 1978) Jan Vaněk is listed as the author of the exhibition "Civilisovaná žena",

noted here as "furniture producer, designer of interiors, furniture, and interior furnishings, publicist."

66) In the article "Civilisovaná žena" (Lidové noviny 1930), Josef Čapek literally writes: "Those proposing this reform, Jan Vaněk and B. Horneková, are leaving..", etc. In the publication "Civilisovaná žena", however, only "prof. B. Horneková" is expressly mentioned as the person making these proposals. Additionally, it could also have been the result of cooperation with Zdeněk Rossman, who had close contacts with the Bauhaus and had also studied at the German school between 1928 and 1929. He could have contributed to the idea of a functionalist notion of women's wardrobe (though rather only functional). Nevertheless, as is known, clothes design, let alone fashion creation, was not among the subjects taught at the Bauhaus school.

67) At the end of the 1940s, Josef Vydra — noted pedagogue, popularizer and theoretician of industrial arts — appraised the folkloristic tendency in a brochure called "Svéráz" (Brno 1940) in the following manner: "Elsewhere the word svéráz /folkloristic-trans./ denotes something especially good and well-crafted of good home materials, beautiful characteristic forms, products corresponding to the needs and habits of life of this or that nation! A nation considers as folkloristic something that it wants to show off, as something that is beautiful, characteristic of the nation and the land, something none else has, something which sets the nation above its neighbors...The word "folkloristic" does not mean to remain culturally behind, does not mean to look back to historical dead forms...May the perfection of production, the functionality of shape and beauty become the art and craft of the nation as a whole and lead us higher to the real qualities of a functional and living sense of beauty. May Czech folklorism simply be the high quality of each product and, most of all, of clothing! Let it become the standard of national requirements and the habits of our life! May the high quality and tasteful form of each product be the best Czechoslovak characteristic also for foreigners!" With these words Josef Vydra ended his article "Svéráz a lidový průmysl" (Folklorism and Folk Industry).

68) Traditional and "folkloristic" clothes (decorated with embroidery of pseudo-folk motifs) for summer days and, on occasion, celebrations remained in the wardrobes of many women and children until the turn of the 1950s and were again worn (blouses, shirts, boleros) in the 1970s, when there was a wave of ethnic fashion.

69) The writer of the article "Československé módy" (Czechoslovak fashion) unfortunately somewhat confused the geographical and cultural determinants of styles which he evidently had seen and described in the article. According to the writer's description, the borders of Czechoslovakia would have also encompassed Romania.

70) Scheufler, P., Hozák, J.: Krásné časy / Rudolf Bruner - Dvořák, Momentní fotograf. Praha 1995, Grafoprint Neubert.

71) Birgus, V.: Fotograf František Drtikol. Praha 1994, Prostor.

72) ST. J.: Pavlova de la Photo. Eva VII, 1935, no. 22, p. 12.

73) Roegiers, P., Baque, D.: Francois Kollar. Paris 1989, Phillippe Sers éditeur/Vilo.

74) Fastrová, O.: Na chvilku, madame. Eva VIII, 1936, no. 7, p. 25.

75) Elegantní Praha I, 1922, no. 1, p. 3.

76) Gentleman I, 1924, no. 1, p. 1.

77) Vondráčková, J.: Kolem Mileny Jesenské. Praha 1991, pp. 17, 30, etc., 60, 75-77, 81, 89, 105. Černá, J.: Adresát Milena Jesenská. Praha 1991, pp. 33, 41, 61, 63, 66, 74-75, 78, 87-88.

78) Jesenská, M.: Tajemství dobrého vzhledu. Gentleman II, 1925, no. 5, p. 109.

79) Jesenská, M.: Člověk dělá šaty. Praha 1927, p. 5, etc., 23, 54.

80) See Jílková, J.: Soupis textilních časopisů a ročenek v Českých zemích v letech 1787-1982. In: Z dějin textilu. Sv. 4. Ústí nad Orlicí 1983.

81) Ženské listy 1915-1917.

82) Světová moda, „svéráz" a kroje. Moda a vkus I, 1919, no. 1, p. 18.

83) Moda a vkus I, 1919, no. 1, p. 6.

84) Moda a vkus I, 1920, no. 8, p. 8.

85) Elegantní Praha II, 1924, no. 4, p. 50.

86) Pachmayerová, A.: Franc. modní přehlídka pražských vzorkových veletrhů. Modní revue VII, 1927, no. 42, p. 7.

87) Pachmayerová, A.: Modní přehlídka Hany Podoské. Modní revue VII, 1927, no. 41, p. 7.

88) Greyová, D.: Eva patří opět Adamovi. Eva I, 1928/29, no. 18, p. 17.

89) Worth, J. Ch.: Co budeme letos nosit. Eva III, 1931, no. 8, p. 17.

90) Jílovská, S.: Podzimní kostymy. Eva III, 1931, pp. 14-15.

91) Jílovská, S.: Do práce. Eva III, 1931, pp. 10-11

92) Sedláková, H.: Málo, ale dobře, je více než mnoho. Eva VII, 1934, no. 1, p. 26.

93) Jílovská, S.: Pro večer. Eva IV, 1932, no. 1, p. 14.

94) Naše anketa. Eva III, 1931, no. 11, p. 13.

95) Dobrý odbyt IV, Dvůr Králové 1933, no. 4.

96) Eva VIII, 1936, no. 11, pp. 18-19.

97) Moravcová, M.: Svérázové tisky firmy Josef Sochor ve Dvoře Králové n. L. /1921-1941/. Český lid LXXVII, 1990, no. 4, pp. 211-219.

98) Pánský šatník. Gentleman VI, 1929, no. 5, p. 114.

99) Páni v cylindrech. Měsíc VII, 1939, no. 3, p. 13.

Elegantní oblek
pro
odpoledne.

Při volbě elegantního obleku pro odpoledne, jež chceme nositi v teplejších dnech, nutno se říditi jiným směrem než při obleku na zimu. Není určen

K 3076. Šaty z vln. lát. a hedvábí.
M 957. Plášť z téhož materiálu. Stř. vel. I., II., III. dodá adm. po 8 Kč.

K 3077. Jumprové šaty z bílého čínského krepu.
M 958. Plášť z bílé kashy. Stř. vel. I., II., III. dodá adm. po 8 Kč.

S 1016. Vycház. oblek z modré vln. látky s vestou. Střih na Střihové příloze.

Modní svět 1926

Selection of literature

Bond D.: The Guiness Guide to 20th Century Fashion, London 1981

Jílková J.: Soupis textilních časopisů a ročenek v Českých zemích v letech 1787 — 1982, in: Z dějin textilu. Studie a materiály, vol. 4, Ústí nad Orlicí 1983

Kybalová J., Lamarová M.: Oděvní tvorba, Prague 1986

Buxbaum G.: Mode aus Wien, Vienna 1986

Herald J.: Fashion of a Decade. The 1920s, London 1991

Vondráčková J.: Kolem Mileny Jesenské, Prague 1991

Constantine M.: Fashion of a Decade. The 1930s, London 1994

Nová encyklopedie výtvarného umění, Prague 1995

Epilogue

Anyone, who can decipher from a town, its streets and structures, not only its history but also the way of living of the past generations, is surely not surprised by the fact that Prague of the 1920s and 1930s also had tailoring houses. It was thanks to these houses that people in the region began speaking of "Prague fashion". It was during the interwar period that fashion also gained its institutional form, based on model production of order houses, design and shows, and on the developing media — print, journalism, graphics, and photography. A noteworthy project, "Civilisovaná žena" (Civilized Woman) arose in the culturally rich environment of Brno. The same period provided the professional conditions for the later establishment of the first higher school of fashion design at the School of Decorative Arts in Prague, which thus complemented the middle level education offered in the subject in Brno. It is, nevertheless, hard to believe how little has thus far been published about fashion of the First Republic and how difficult it still is to gain dependable information in this area.

In its greatest demands, fashion is connected with the lifestyle of the richest classes of society. It was in this connection that it always bore the results of revolutionary changes. The political revolution of 1948 accompanied by the liquidation of the bourgeois and capitalist enterprise disrupted the prospering industry of Czech fashion. Small businessmen and tradesmen found them-selves degraded to undesired professions and were exposed to repression of the most various kind; firm archives disappeared to who knows where; fashion houses were nationalized, several were closed, and others were renamed and changed to fit the new conditions. The following long search for a "new socialist fashion" and "workers' apparel" for a long time also complicated the notion of "western" with regard to "bourgeois and capitalistic" fashion and removed moments of preserved work. A generation of direct experience gradually disappeared and individual works — clothes, accessories — and, in the difficult war- and post-war conditions, usually ended in trashcans after several mendings.

This publication, the first of its kind, is being published on the occasion of the exhibition of Czech fashion 1918-1939 taking place in the Fall 1996 in the Museum of Decorative Arts in Prague. It does not intend nor, as already noted, is not able to provide a complete picture of fashion of this period, and thus cannot fill in the gaps of our knowledge regarding Czech fashion production. It only attempts to demarcate the first contours of this period — the basic interconnnections and influences, determining personalities, method of production, areas of distribution and particular character of fashion of this period.

The sources used for the difficult historical reconstruction were, first and foremost, contemporary magazines and fashion collections of the Museum of Decorative Arts in Prague — a collection which, as one of the museum's youngest, was systematically built up starting in the 1960s.

In several cases the authors also have drawn on personal reminiscences and oral histories, whose reliability will perhaps be shown by future research. This decisive period of Czech fashion would undoubtedly be well served by specific research — research which this exhibition and publication would like in its way to initiate.
E. U., H. J.

58

59

91058

91059

91060

91061

60

61

Dámské Modní Listy 1920

The Museum of Decorative Arts in Prague

The foundation of the Museum of Decorative Arts in Prague in 1885 reflected the rapid development of Czech society at this time. The museum soon became a well-known cultural and educational center in the territory of what was then still the Czech Crown lands of the Austro-Hungarian Empire.

The unfavourable influence of the industrial revolution on the aesthetic side and, with this, also on the quality of production had already been the subject of criticism of artists, theoreticians and the general public. The idea of establishing a permanent exhibition of arts and crafts in Prague was already contained in the exhibition organized by the Arkadia association in 1861 in the Old Town city hall in Prague. In 1868 the Prague Chamber of Trade and Commerce together with the Viennese Museum of Art and Industry organized an exhibition in the Žofín of objects that had been acquired at the World Exhibition in Paris in 1867, supplemented by hi-storical works of arts and crafts that were primarily from the collection of Vojtěch Lanna (the later well-known donor and supporter of the museum). The offer of the exhibition spaces in the Rudolfinum (House of Artists), given in 1867 and brought into realization in 1885, contributed to the creation of the new museum at a time when financial means and space had not yet been found. In 1885, the board of the Chamber of Trade and Commerce in Prague decided to establish an independent museum. A neo-renaissance museum building was built between 1897 and 1900 according to a design by Professor of Architecture Josef Schulz on a site between the Old Jewish cemetery and a street at the edge of the Josefov section of the city.

At present the museum has at its disposal four exhibition halls for permanent exhibits (since 1985) displaying world-class objects of arts and crafts from the 16th through the middle of the 19th century; one exhibition hall for temporary exhibits (4-6 per year); and permanent exhibits at five chateaus — Klášterec, Duchcov, Hrubý Rohozec, Lemberk and Doudleby. The museum also organizes and co-organizes many exhibitions outside the museum building.

A specialized museum library (the only of its kind in the Czech Republic) with an extensive collection of books and publications is open to the public. The library offers its services for the exchange of publications, research, and xerox copying.

Some 80% of the total of more than 200,000 objects in the museum's collection are contained in the depositaries of the collections, which are divided into four departments (I. collections of glass, porcelain and ceramics; II. collections of applied graphics and photographs; III. collection of furniture, work of wood, metals and various materials; IV. collections of textiles, fashion and toys).

In the year 2000, when Prague is celebrated as European cultural metropolis, the museum would like to present itself in modernized form on a European level for the enjoyment of all visitors to the city.

Madame **TOMBO**

se vrátila z Paříže a Londýna a přivezla nové překrásné modely dámských kloboučků. Dovoluje si Vás milostivá tímto pozvat k jich přehlídce.

Modelový dům dámských klobouků.
Praha, Václavské nám. 12. ● Tel. 38.207. ● Lift

Czech Fashion

1918

1939

Elegance of the Czechoslovak First Republic

Co-authors: PhDr. Helena Jarošová,
PhDr. Josef Kroutvor, Jan Mlčoch
and Petr Štembera
English translation: Štěpán Suchochleb
and Andreas Beckmann
Photography: Miloslav Šebek and archives
of the Museum of Decorative Arts in Prague
Typography: Clara Istlerová

EVA UCHALOVÁ

Published by Olympia a.s., Klimentská 1, Prague 1
in cooperation with Museum of Decorative Arts in
Prague in 1996 as its 2822nd publication
First print, 120 pages
Editor: Marie Průšová
Lithography: Studio TYPO, spol. s r.o.
Drtinova 2, Praha 5
Printed by Svoboda a.s.
Sazečská 8, Praha 10
Tem.sk. 02
27-033-96

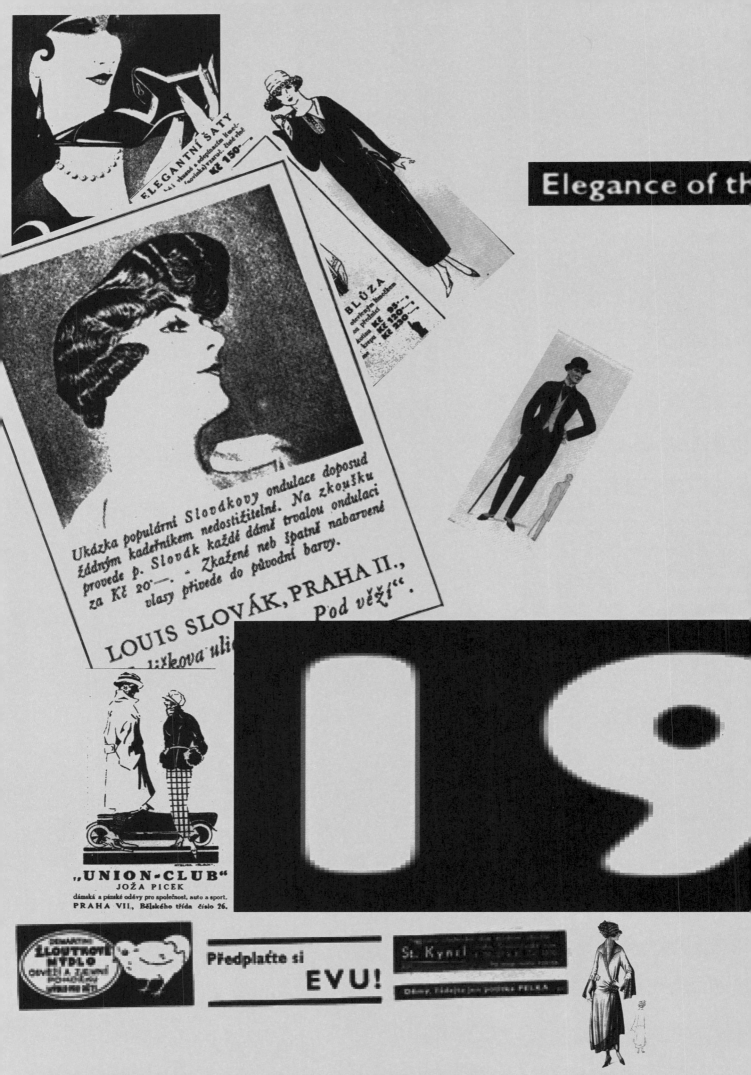